# SURVIVE THE SAVAGE SEA

# for Anne

Penguin Books Ltd, Harmondsworth,
Middlesex, England
Penguin Books Australia Ltd, Ringwood,
Victoria, Australia
Penguin Books (N.Z.) Ltd,
182-190 Wairau Road, Auckland 10, New Zealand

First published by Elek 1973
Published in Penguin Books for sale outside the United Kingdom 1974
Published in Penguin Books for sale within the United Kingdom 1975

Copyright © Dougal Robertson, 1973
Drawings by Pam Littlewood, copyright
© Elek Books Ltd, 1973

Made and printed in Great Britain by
Hazell Watson & Viney Ltd
Aylesbury, Bucks
Set in Monotype Baskerville

Penguin Books
Survive the Savage Seas

Dougal Robertson was born in Edinburgh in 1924. He served with the Merchant Marine from 1941; after war service he spent most of the remainder of his seafaring career in the Far East. He met his wife (then a Sister in the Colonial Nursing Service) in Hong Kong, where they were married in 1951. After taking his Master's Certificate he left the sea to farm in North Staffordshire. In 1970 he sold up and purchased *Lucette* to take his family on an educational cruise round the world.

Dougal Robertson

Penguin Books

# Contents

# List of Illustrations

*Drawings by Pam Littlewood*

# Author's Acknowledgements

I should like to thank my sister Alison Quinn for her encouragement and research; Lizzie Jackson for her help; and Mr Kashiwa Yoshito for the use of the photograph reproduced on pages 168–9. Grateful thanks are also due to the Hakluyt Society and Cambridge University Press for their permission to quote passages from Richard Hakluyt's *Principall Navigations, Voiages and Discoveries of the English Nation* and from Captain Cook's *Journals* . . . edited by J. C. Beaglehole, Volume III: *The Voyage of the Resolution and Discovery 1776–1780.*

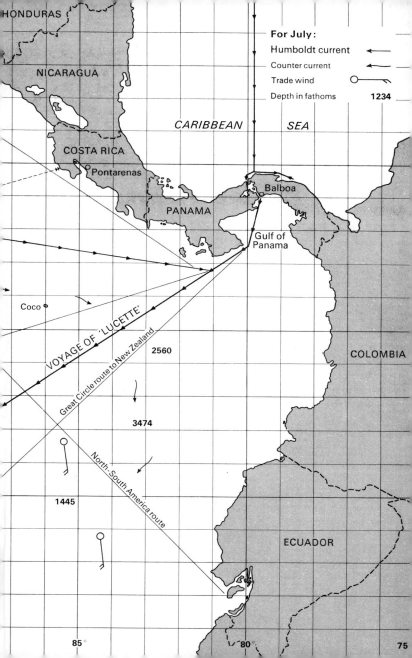

# Glossary of Sailing Terms

Broach to: To turn accidentally sideways into strong wind and sea

Dead reckoning: Estimation of position from course steered and distance run

Drogue: Pocket of fabric to reduce movement of a raft or boat in strong winds

Fo'c'stle: Cabin nearest the bows

Freeboard: Distance from the water to the top of the side of a boat

Garboard strake: The hull plank next to the keel

Genoa: Large sail used in light winds

Grommet: Circle of rope

Gunwhale: Top of the side of a boat

Leeway: Drift due to wind

Luff: Leading part of a sail

Reef: To reduce the sail area

Schooner: Sailing vessel with fore and aft rig and mainmast nearest the stern; *Lucette* was a Staysail schooner

Sea anchor: Device to restrict leeway (q.v.), in the form of a water parachute

Set: Direction (of current)

Sheet: Rope attached to lower corner or corners of sail used to extend sail or alter its direction

Stays: Supports for mast

Swell: Waves caused by distant winds

Thole pins: Upright supports to which an oar may be attached

Trim: Manner in which a vessel floats in the water: distribution of centre of gravity in relation to centre of buoyancy

Yaw: To turn sideways

# Prologue

It was a Sunday morning in the autumn of the year 1968. As I watched the milk wagon pull out of the yard on its morning collection round I sighed resignedly and walked slowly towards the farmhouse; yields were down again but fifteen years on an upland dairy farm in North Staffordshire had tempered my enthusiasm for an agricultural way of life, changing an interest in progressive farming techniques into a grim determination to endure the deterioration in living standards which had reduced the number of small dairy producers in England by fifty per cent in the preceding ten years.

The cobbled road wound round the back of the farmhouse. I turned and glanced back across the concrete surround to the cowsheds, now converted to modern yard and parlour milking, then back to the square unpretentious farmhouse, grey green lichen mellowing the red sandstone to give the thick three-hundred-year-old walls the appearance of having grown from the soil rather than having been built upon it. I crossed the stone flags fronting the house, and as I opened the door to the kitchen, the children's voices filtered in high-pitched chatter from the upstairs bedrooms. During the week, my wife Lyn commuted the six miles to the market town of Leek by motorised cycle to carry out her duties as midwifery sister in the small maternity unit, but on Sunday she took one of her two days 'off duty' to be at home with the children during their weekend's holiday from school. Sunday had evolved, not so much as a day of rest for the Robertson family as a day of family communion when the previous week's happenings were recounted and the coming week's plans discussed, a day for visits from friends and relatives and for lying abed late, except for Dad who had the privilege of rising early to pursue his chosen way of life, along with seventy thousand other servile dairymen around the country.

As I look back on those memories of our life on the farm it is

difficult to prevent an idyllic air of rustic content from masking
the gnawing worries of financial burdens, the hard unyielding
routine of farm labour which had allowed me fourteen days'
holiday in fifteen years, and the discontent which results from
the frustration of seeing hopes and visions crumble under the
crude realities of economic necessity. That Sunday morning
stands out clearly in my memory, however, as one of the nice
days. I had put the kettle on the hot plate of the solid fuel
cooker and while waiting for it to boil switched on the radio to
listen to the news, which contained a commentary on the
Round the World yacht race. I had carried the mugs of tea
upstairs on a tray, calling to Anne, our sixteen-year-old daughter, to come through to our room where nine-year-old twins
Neil and Sandy rocked with laughter as they lay in bed with
their mother watching our son Douglas perform one of his
special slapstick comedy acts. As Douglas rolled his eyes and
cavorted round the bedroom in stiff-legged imitation of a
disabled robot, Neil's face reddened as he laughed all the
breath from his lungs, and even the more serious-minded Sandy
chuckled in ecstasy as he watched his fifteen-year-old brother's
antics.

Anne followed me into the bedroom, yawning widely, her
long golden hair in tumbled profusion on the shoulders of her
dressing gown. She thumped Douglas with her fist in passing
and jumped quickly into bed beside her mother as Douglas
made to retaliate, then slowly their laughter quietened as we
talked of school, of Douglas's rugger, of Anne's rock-climbing,
of the twins' new teacher, until finally we came round to the
world yacht race. They listened interestedly as I told them of
the dangers and the privations which faced these lone yachts-
men in mid-ocean, finding it difficult to describe the hostile
character of an ocean environment to youngsters who had been
no further than the sea shore and whose conception of a large
stretch of water approximated to the local reservoir.

Neil and Sandy had become silent while Anne and Douglas
questioned and Lyn talked of our sailing adventures in Hong
Kong before we had started farming, but suddenly Neil
shouted 'Daddy's a sailor, why can't we go round the world?'
Lyn burst out laughing and 'What a lovely idea!' she ex-
claimed, 'Let's buy a boat and go round the world.' I realised

that Neil, who thought Manchester was one of the four brown corners of the earth, had no conception of the meaning of his remark, and that his mother was entering into the spirit of the game, but suddenly, to me, it was no game. Why not? I looked at Anne and Douglas, both handsome children but the horizons of their minds stunted by the limitations of their environment. In two years they would both have reached school leaving age and neither had shown any leaning towards academic aptitude, and the twins, already backward compared with their contemporaries in town, were unlikely to blossom into sudden educational prodigies. In two years' time they would finish their primary schooling and then . . . Why not indeed?

We were reasonably well qualified to undertake such a voyage. In my twelve years at sea, I had gained a Foreign Going Master Mariner's certificate, Lyn was a practising midwife and a State Registered Nurse with additional qualifications in fever nursing. She could make herself understood in rather rusty Arabic and Cantonese while I could stumble along in equally rusty Hindustani and French. After fifteen years of hard living as ungentlemanly farmers we were in tough physical condition and the children had a good background of practical training in helping with the farmwork.

Two years later, after selling our entire holdings in stock and land, we had acquired enough money to embark on the initial stage of our planned circumnavigation of the world.

The fifty-year-old, nineteen-ton, forty-three-foot schooner *Lucette* had been purchased in Malta and subjected to a rigorous survey, any suspect hull planking was renewed and all the surveyor's recommendations were carried out. Anne and I had flown to Malta and with the help of two friends we sailed *Lucette* back to Britain through some rough weather in November Biscay, sustaining a knockdown and a broken boom on the way, but arriving in Falmouth full of confidence in the seaworthiness of our craft. We stayed two months in Falmouth where Lyn, Douglas and the twins became accustomed to shipboard life while *Lucette* was fitted with a new main boom, and had some caulking renewed and sails restitched.

We left Falmouth at the end of January 1971, running before

a Northerly which gradually increased to a screaming sixty mile an hour gale off Finisterre six days later. We weathered it out, in mast high waves under bare poles, giving my family as rough an initiation to the sea as any pressed crew of bygone days. Anne was confined to her bunk with 'flu and since we had no self-steering device, Douglas had to fill the gap and he worked opposite me, four hours on, four off with a stoicism and resourcefulness which won our respect and admiration. I know of no more satisfying conceit than the discovery of such hidden depths of character in one's own children.

After a drying out period in Lisbon, we enjoyed fair weather to the Canary Islands. Lyn's sisters, Edna and Mary, flew to Las Palmas to bid us a final farewell and we loaded stores and extra crew in the shape of two young American graduates, Barbara and Steve, who were hitching a lift across the Atlantic. Lyn and I had decided that if possible we would carry students from different countries and walks of life to give our own family a diversion from boring old Mum and Dad, and so we sailed in the wake of Columbus past the Old Man of Tenerife, bucketing around in a fresh northerly gale which left Steve prostrate for a large part of the way across the Atlantic. Barbara on the other hand quickly gained her sea legs and kept the twins (and us adults too) enthralled with her readings from *Winnie the Pooh*.

Now hardened seafarers, we cruised through the Windward Islands of the West Indies in company with some Icelandic friends we had met in Falmouth, going wherever scenic beauty or historic interest led us, then up through the Bahamas where Anne fell in love with a young Canadian, to Miami. The hurricane season was upon us so we stayed in Miami where the twins and Douglas caught up on some school work. It was while we were in Miami that we purchased our fibreglass dinghy from a Mr Stuart of Fort Lauderdale, and admiring its stout lines and the good quality of the workmanship, Lyn remarked how our lives might depend on it one day. We named it *Ednamair* after Lyn's sisters.

In February 1972 Anne decided to stay in Nassau and pursue her own destiny so we made our way rather sadly to Jamaica, a beautiful island full of friendly people. We climbed the 7,400 foot Blue Mountain Peak to celebrate Douglas's

*Above:* The Robertson family before setting out from Falmouth.
*Left to right:* Douglas, Neil, Lyn, Sandy, the author, Anne. *Below:*
Lucette off the coast of Jamaica, *en route* for Panama

eighteenth birthday and learned much of the Jamaican way
of life from friends in Port Antonio, finally sailing for the San
Blas Islands with an extra crew member, Scott, who cruised
this idyllic archipelago with us and returned home from Colon
in Panama.

Robin Williams, a twenty-two-year-old Welsh graduate in
economics and statistics, joined us in Panama for the voyage to
New Zealand. His cheerful smiling visage and adventurous
spirit made him stand out amongst his bored, unhappy, introspective contemporaries, and as parents we hoped that a little
of his arithmetical prowess would rub off on our twins. Our
passage through the Panama Canal for a very modest fee was
fascinating to the boys as the enormous locks passed us from
one ocean to the other.

We anchored off the US Quarantine Zone that May night;
the following morning we weighed anchor and sailed south-
west into the Bay of Panama, the offshore breeze making for
easy sailing in pleasant conditions. Bright golden sea snakes,
undulating their three foot length in the blue seas, looked too
pretty to be highly poisonous which I am told they are and the
myriads of seabirds, from stately frigate birds, gulls and terns
to the tiny petrels, held our interest as we cruised past the coastal
farmlands of Panama and out into the long rolling swells of
the Pacific Ocean *en route* for the Galapagos Islands.

Part One

# The Attack

The black volcanic mountain of Fernandina, the most westerly of the Galapagos Islands, towered high above the tall masts of the schooner *Lucette* as she lay at anchor, rolling gently in the remnants of the long Pacific swell which surged round the rocky headland of Cape Espinosa, and sent searching fingers of white surf curling into the sheltered waters of the anchorage.

We had spent a pleasant morning sailing across the strait from Tagus cove, on Isabela Island, where Douglas, accompanied by Neil and Sandy, had carefully recorded *Lucette*'s name and registry amongst the impressive array of names of yachts and fishing vessels which had visited the cove over the past fifty years. The names, painted on the cliff sides of the cove in two-feet-high letters, gave the anchorage an atmosphere of gaiety and companionship which lingered on after we had left the sun-sparkled waters of the cove, and seemed reflected in the joyous antics of the seals and dolphins as they escorted us into the strait. Now, however, as gathering clouds obscured the sun, we shivered in the slightly sinister atmosphere of Espinosa, where we hoped to see the Galapagos penguins and the flightless cormorants disporting themselves in factual support of Darwin's *Origin of Species*.

The black volcanic sand of the beaches, the jagged fangs of black rock jutting out from the headland, the rather scruffy appearance of the birds, so sleek and beautiful on the other islands, all lent this air of depression to Espinosa, so that it was without our usual feelings of interest and wonder that we saw half a dozen penguins grouped at the water's edge ready to take to the water at our near approach.

Robin peered anxiously through his spectacles at the lens of his camera to take a rather distant photograph of the penguins, then muttered darkly as he moved closer to a better vantage

Flightless Cormorant

point, causing the penguins to plop neatly one by one into the sea and disappear. I walked with him, past the loathsome piles of black marine iguanas and the scarlet shells of the rock crabs to where my wife Lyn searched the rock pools for additions to her shell collection; a white-crested crane walked with dignified gait on the nearby rocks quietly ignoring us as it scanned the small pools, while pelicans flapped their ungainly wings over-head, suddenly changing shape to streamlined projectiles as they hunted their prey in the cloudy waters of the bay.

We had passed the bloated body of a dead seal on our way in, with the sinister triangular-shaped fin of a white-tipped shark near by, so I told the lads to keep close inshore if they wanted to swim. As it was, only Douglas had ventured into the water and even he, intrepid reef explorer that he was, had come ashore when a seal, covered with boils, had poked a belligerent snout at him.

Marine Iguana

As we rowed back to *Lucette* in our small fibreglass dinghy we felt rather disappointed at this anticlimax to our journey around these wonderful equatorial islands, with their strange anachronisms of wildlife.

We were on the eve of our departure for the Marquesas Islands, three thousand miles to the west, and now, as the wind swung to the east under a grey mantle of rain cloud, I felt anxious to be gone, for if we left now we would be out from under the lee of the island by morning. Lyn protested vehemently at the thought of starting our journey on June the thirteenth, even when I pointed out that the most superstitious of seafarers didn't mind so long as it wasn't a Friday as well, but Douglas and Robin both now joined with my feelings of anxiety to be gone, and after a short spell of intense activity, we stowed and lashed the dinghy and secured all movables on deck and below.

By five o'clock in the afternoon we were ready for sea, and with mainsail and jibs set we heaved the anchor home, reached past the headland into the strait, then altering course to the west ran free towards the Pacific, a thousand square feet of sail billowing above *Lucette* as she moved easily along the ragged black coastline of Fernandina towards the largest stretch of ocean in the world.

*Lucette* had no self-steering device, and so with night watches arranged, we sailed quietly through the darkness, crossing the sheltered stretch of water in the lee of the massive bulk of the extinct volcano, until at three-thirty in the morning, booms were swung over, stays and sheets hauled taut and secured as the schooner heeled, gently at first, then with steeply inclined decks as she reached across the increasing force of the southerly trade winds at a steady seven knots. By the morning of the fourteenth, the Galapagos Islands were receding into the distance astern, merging with the clouds of the overcast sky above as *Lucette*, now rolling and pitching in the heavy swell and rough seas of the Pacific trades, made steady progress west by south towards the Marquesas Islands.

In spite of the fact that we had been sailing for over a year, our stomachs still took a little time to adjust from the quietness of sheltered waters to the lively movement of the yacht in the open sea and so throughout the day those of us not actively engaged in steering and sailing *Lucette* rested as best we could in the bunks below, supplied at intervals with hot soup or coffee from Lyn's indomitable labours at the stove. Unused to the sea, Robin had been sick most of the way from Panama to the Galapagos, but he now seemed better adjusted to the physical discomfort of the constant heave of the hull. He was able to steer a fairly accurate course by compass, and although the principles of sailing were still something of a closed book to him, he could help Douglas and me with the night watches whilst Lyn and the twins helped with the watches during the day.

The wind moderated a little during the following night and breaks in the cloud enabled us to catch glimpses of stars in the pre-dawn sky; on the morning of the fifteenth we had our first glimpse of the sun since leaving the Galapagos and with the slackening of wind and speed *Lucette* settled to a more comfortable movement in the diminishing seas.

The morning sun shone fitfully from the thinning cloud, and as I balanced myself against the surge of *Lucette*'s deck, sextant glued to my eye, I watched for the right moment when the image of the sun's rim would tip the true horizon, no easy combination when both deck and horizon are in constant motion. Douglas and Sandy were in the cockpit, one steering and the other tending the fishing line, while Robin, finding it difficult to sleep in his

own bunk on the port side of the main cabin, had nipped
quietly into Sandy's bunk on the starboard side of the fo'c'stle
to rest after his spell on the four to eight morning watch. Neil
was reading a book in his own bunk on the port side of the
fo'c'stle, and Lyn had just started to clean up the usual chaos
which results from a rough stretch of sailing. At last the sun,
the horizon and the deck cooperated to give me a fairly accurate
reading, and noting the local time by my watch at $09^h 54^m 45^s$,
I collected my logarithm tables and Nautical Almanac from the
chart table and retired below to the relative comfort of the after
cabin to work out our longitude; it was my first position sight
since leaving the islands.

With my sextant carefully replaced in its box I had turned
to my books to work up a reasonably accurate dead-reckoning
position when sledgehammer blows of incredible force struck
the hull beneath my feet hurling me against the bunk, the noise
of the impact almost deafening my ears to the roar of inrushing
water. I heard Lyn call out, and almost at the same time heard
the cry of 'Whales!' from the cockpit. My senses still reeled as
I dropped to my knees and tore up the floorboards to gaze in
horror at the blue Pacific through the large splintered hole
punched up through the hull planking between two of the
grown oak frames. Water was pouring up through the hole with
torrential force and although Lyn called out that it was no use,
that the water was pouring in from another hole under the
WC flooring as well, I jammed my foot on the broken strakes
and shouted to her to give me large cloths, anything to stem
the flood. She threw me a pillow and I jammed it down on top
of the broken planking, rammed the floorboard on top and
stood on it; the roar of the incoming water scarcely diminished,
it was already above the level of the floorboards as I heard
Douglas cry from the deck 'Are we sinking, Dad?' 'Yes!
Abandon ship!'; my voice felt remote as numbly I watched the
water rise rapidly up the engine casing; it was lapping my knees
as I turned to follow Lyn, already urging Neil and Robin on deck.

Wading past the galley stove, my eye glimpsed the sharp
vegetable knife, and grabbing it in passing I leapt for the
companionway; the water, now up to my thighs, was already
lapping the top of the batteries in the engine room; it was my
last glimpse of *Lucette*'s interior, our home for nearly eighteen

months. Lyn was tying the twins' lifejackets on with rapid
efficiency as I slashed at the lashings holding the bow of the
dinghy to the mainmast; Douglas struggled to free the self-
inflatable raft from under the dinghy and I ran forward to cut
the remaining lashings holding the stern of the dinghy to the
foremast, lifting the dinghy and freeing the raft at the same
time. Lyn shouted for the knife to free the water containers and
I threw it towards her; Douglas again shouted to me if he should
throw the raft over, disbelieving that we were really sinking.
'Yes, get on with it!' I yelled, indicating to Robin, who now had
his lifejacket on, to help him. Grasping the handles at the stern
of the dinghy, I twisted it over from its inverted stowed position
and slid it towards the rail, noting that the water was now
nearly level with *Lucette*'s deck as she wallowed sluggishly in the
seaway. Douglas ran from the after deck with the oars and
thrust them under the thwarts as I slid the dinghy seawards
across the coach roof, then he took hold of the stern from me and
slid the dinghy the rest of the way into the sea, Robin holding
on to the painter to keep it from floating away. The raft, to our
relief, our great and lasting relief, had gone off with a bang and
was already half-inflated, and Lyn, having severed the lashings
on the water containers and flares, was carrying them to the
dinghy. I caught up the knife and again shouted 'Abandon
ship!' for I feared *Lucette*'s rigging might catch one of us as she
went down, then cut the lashings on a bag of onions, which I gave
to Sandy, instructing him to make for the raft, a bag of oranges
which I threw into the dinghy and a small bag of lemons to
follow. It was now too dangerous to stay aboard, and noting
that Douglas, Robin and Sandy had already gone and that Neil
was still sitting in the dinghy which was three-quarters full of
water, I shouted that he also should make for the raft. He
jumped back on *Lucette*, clutching his teddy bears, then plunged
into the sea, swimming strongly for the raft. Lyn struggled
through the rails into the water, still without a lifejacket, and
I walked into the sea, first throwing the knife into the dinghy,
the waters closing over *Lucette*'s scuppers as we left her.

I feared that the whales would now attack us and urged
everyone into the raft, which was fully inflated and exhausting
surplus gas noisily. After helping Lyn into the raft I swam back
to the dinghy, now completely swamped, with oranges floating

around it from the bag which had burst, and standing inside it to protect myself from attack, threw all the oranges and lemons within reach into the raft. The water containers had already floated away or had sunk, as had the box of flares, and since the dinghy was now three feet under the water, having only enough flotation to support itself, I made my way back to the raft again, grabbing a floating tin of petrol as I went. On leaving the dinghy I caught a last glimpse of *Lucette*, the water level with her spreaders and only the tops of her sails showing. Slowly she curtsied below the waves, a lady to the last; she was gone when I looked again.

I climbed wearily into the yellow inflatable, a sense of un-reality flooding through me, feeling sure that soon I would waken and find the dream gone. I looked at my watch; it was one minute to ten. 'Killer whales,' said Douglas. 'All sizes, about twenty of them. Sandy saw one with a big V in its head. I think three of them hit us at once.' My mind refused to take in the implications of the attack; I gazed at the huge genoa sail lying on the raft floor where Lyn was sitting with the twins. 'How the hell did that get there?' I asked stupidly. Douglas grinned. 'I saw the fishing line spool floating on the surface unwinding itself,' he said, 'so I grabbed it and pulled it in, the sail was hooked in the other end!'

Three killer whales; I remembered the one in captivity in Miami Seaquarium weighed three tons and that they swam at about thirty knots into an attack; no wonder the holes in *Lucette*! The others had probably eaten the injured one with the V in its head, which must have split its skull when it hit *Lucette*'s three-ton lead keel. She had served us well to the very end, and now she was gone.

Lyn gazed numbly at me, quietly reassuring the twins who had started crying, and, apart from the noise of the sea round us, we gazed in silent disbelief at our strange surroundings.

# Part Two

# Castaways

We sat on the salvaged pieces of flotsam lying on the raft floor, our faces a pale bilious colour under the bright yellow canopy, and stared at each other, the shock of the last few minutes gradually seeping through to our consciousness. Neil, his teddy bears gone, sobbed in accompaniment to Sandy's hiccup cry, while Lyn repeated the Lord's Prayer, then, comforting them, sang the hymn 'For those in peril on the Sea'. Douglas and Robin watched at the doors of the canopy to retrieve any useful pieces of debris which might float within reach and gazed with dumb longing at the distant five-gallon water container, bobbing its polystyrene lightness ever further away from us in the steady trade wind. The dinghy *Ednamair* wallowed, swamped, near-by with a line attached to it from the raft and our eyes travelled over and beyond to the heaving undulations of the horizon, already searching for a rescue ship even while knowing there would not be one. Our eyes travelled fruitlessly across the limitless waste of sea and sky, then once more ranged over the scattering debris. Of the killer whales which had so recently shattered our very existence, there was no sign. Lyn's sewing basket floated close and it was brought aboard followed by a couple of empty boxes, the canvas raft cover, and a plastic cup.

I leaned across to Neil and put my arm round him, 'It's alright now, son, we're safe and the whales have gone.' He looked at me reproachfully. 'We're not crying 'cos we're frightened,' he sobbed, 'we're crying 'cos Lucy's gone.' Lyn gazed at me over their heads, her eyes filling with tears. 'Me too,' she said, and after a moment added, 'I suppose we'd better find out how we stand.'

This was the question I had been dreading; feelings of guilt, that our present predicament was not only due to my unortho-dox ideas on educating our children (there had been plenty of critics to object that I was needlessly jeopardising the children's lives) but also that I had failed to foresee this type of disaster,

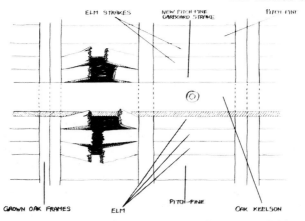

Damage to *Lucette*'s hull from one Killer Whale, a fatal blow in itself. She was struck by three

now engulfed me, and this, added to the fact that we had lost almost everything we possessed as well as *Lucette*, depressed me to the depths of despair. How could I have been so foolish as to trust our lives to such an old schooner! Then I saw, once again, in my mind's eye that damage under the floorboards of *Lucette*. Not only had the frames withstood the impact of the blow, but the new garboard strake of inch and a half pitchpine, fitted in Malta at the surveyor's recommendation, had been one of the hull planks which had been smashed inwards. Her hull had taken a full minute to sink below the waves, but a modern boat, constructed with less regard to brute strength than *Lucette*, would have sustained much heavier damage and sunk even more quickly, with more terrible results.

I looked at Douglas, he had grown to manhood in our eighteen months at sea together; the twins, previously shy, introspective farm lads, had become interested in the different peoples we had met and their various ways of life, and were now keen to learn more; I tried to ease my conscience with the thought that they had derived much benefit from their voyage and that our sinking was as unforeseeable as an earthquake, or an aeroplane crash, or anything to ease my conscience.

We cleared a space on the floor and opened the survival kit, which was part of the raft's equipment, and was contained in a three-foot-long polythene cylinder; slowly we took stock:

Vitamin fortified bread and glucose for ten men for two days.

Eighteen pints of water, eight flares (two parachute, six hand).

One bailer, two large fish-hooks, two small, one spinner and trace and a twenty-five pound breaking strain fishing line.

A patent knife which would not puncture the raft (or anything else for that matter), a signal mirror, torch, first-aid box, two sea anchors, instruction book, bellows, and three paddles.

In addition to this there was the bag of a dozen onions which I had given to Sandy, to which Lyn had added a one-pound tin of biscuits and a bottle containing about half a pound of glucose sweets, ten oranges and six lemons. How long would this have to last us? As I looked round our meagre stores my heart sank and it must have shown on my face for Lyn put her hand on mine; 'We must get these boys to land,' she said quietly. 'If we do nothing else with our lives, we must get them to land!' I looked at her and nodded, 'Of course, we'll make it!' The answer came from my heart but my head was telling me a different story. We were over two hundred miles down wind and current from the Galapagos Islands. To try to row the small dinghy into two hundred miles of rough ocean weather was an impossible journey even if it was tried by only two of us in an attempt to seek help for the others left behind in the raft. The fact that the current was against us as well only put the seal of hopelessness on the idea. There was no way back.

The Marquesas Islands lay two thousand eight hundred miles to the west but we had no compass or means of finding our position; if, by some miraculous feat of endurance, one of us made the distance the chances of striking an island were remote.

The coast of Central America, more than a thousand miles to the north-east, lay on the other side of the windless Doldrums, that dread area of calms and squalls which had inspired Coleridge's

> Water, water, everywhere,
> And all the boards did shrink;
> Water, water, everywhere,
> Nor any drop to drink.

I was a Master Mariner, I thought ruefully, not an ancient
one, and could count on no ghostly crew to get me out of this
dilemma!

What were our chances if we followed the textbook answer,
'Stay put and wait for rescue?' In the first place we wouldn't
be missed for at least five weeks and if a search was made, where
would they start looking in three thousand miles of ocean? In
the second place the chance of seeing a passing vessel in this
area was extremely remote and could be discounted completely,
for of the two possible shipping routes from Panama to Tahiti and
New Zealand, one lay four hundred miles to the south and the
other three hundred miles to the north. Looking at the food, I
estimated that six of us might live for ten days and since we
could expect no rain in this area for at least six months, apart
from an odd shower, our chances of survival beyond ten days
were doubtful indeed. It seemed to me that we stood a very good
chance of becoming one of Robin's statistics.

My struggle to reach a decision, gloomy whichever way I
looked at it, showed on my face, and Lyn leaned forward. 'Tell
us how we stand,' she said, looking round, 'we want to know the
truth.' They all nodded, 'What chance have we?' I could not
tell them I thought they were going to die so I slowly spelled
out the alternatives, and then suddenly I knew there was only
one course open to us; we must sail with the trade winds to the
Doldrums four hundred miles to the north. We stood a thin
chance of reaching land but the only possible shipping route
lay in that direction, our only possible chance of rain water in
any quantity lay in that direction even if it was four hundred
miles away, and our only possible chance of reaching land lay
in that direction, however small that chance might be. We
would work and fight for our lives at least; better than dying in
idleness! 'We must get these boys to land,' Lyn had said. I felt
the reality of the decision lifting the hopelessness from my
shoulders and looked around; five pairs of eyes watched me as
I spoke, Lyn once again with her arms round the twins,
Douglas and Robin each at their lookout posts watching for any
useful debris that might come within reach. 'We have no
alternative,' I said, 'we'll stay here for twenty-four hours to see
if any other wreckage appears, then we must head north and
hope to find rain in the Doldrums.' I looked round, 'We might

also find an easterly current there which will help us to the coast of Central America, if we've not been picked up by then.' The lifting of my depression communicated and as I talked of the problems and privations which confronted us, I saw the resolve harden on Douglas's face. Robin nodded and fired a question about shipping lanes, Lyn smiled at me, not caring that I was offering her torture from thirst, starvation and probably death if we were not rescued, just so long as we had a working chance. The twins dried their tears and eyed the sweets; we were in business again.

With one of the sea anchors streamed we set to work, clearing the raft floor of the debris we had collected: the huge genoa sail, two hundred feet of nylon fishing line (breaking strain one hundred pounds), three gallons of petrol, two oars, two empty boxes. Lyn's sewing basket was a treasure beyond wealth for not only did it contain the usual threads and needles, but also two scalpel blades, four knitting needles, a blanket pin, hat pin, three plastic bags, a ball of string, buttons, tinfoil, a shoehorn, two small plastic cups, two plastic boxes, two small envelopes of dried yeast, a piece of copper wire one foot long, some elastic, a bottle of soluble aspirin, a pencil, and a biro pen. (What else could one possibly expect to find in a sewing basket!) We also had a half pint of copal varnish, a very sodden edition of a West Indies pilotage book, and one cracked and saturated smoke flare. My watch, a twenty-year-old Rolex Oyster, gave us the time and the first-aid box contained artery forceps and scissors, but otherwise we had no compass, no charts, no instruments of any kind in fact, that would aid our navigation or measure our distance run.

We stowed the mountain of debris as best we could then set to work, our first task being to strip out the long luff wire from the genoa so that it could be used to join the dinghy to the raft. It was at this point that we met our first real drawback for first Robin, then Neil started being seasick, the undulating motion of the raft in the high swell and breaking seas finding them unable to settle to the strange movement. Lyn administered seasick pills from the first-aid box as soon as she thought the boys able to retain them, but they had already lost precious quantities of body fluid. Lyn and I continued to work on the sail while Douglas checked and re-stowed the rations and equipment. In one of the raft pockets he found two sponges and plugs, with a repair kit for holes, but the glue had completely dried out, rendering the repair kit useless. In another pocket he found the instruction book which gave little intelligent information on how to preserve one's life in mid-ocean, but gave a lot of superfluous jargon about morale, leadership, and rescue, finishing up with the two most sensible words in the whole book in capital letters, GOOD LUCK!! (The exclamation marks are mine.)

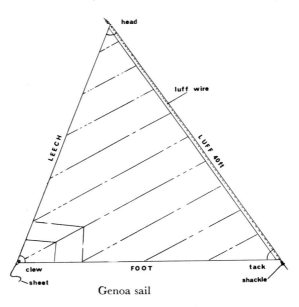

Genoa sail

At last we freed the luff wire, about forty feet long and covered with white plastic, then set about cutting a sail for the dinghy, after which we could use the surplus for sheets and covers for warmth at night, since we were all clad in swimming shorts and shirts with the exception of Lyn, who was wearing a nylon housecoat. The wire would make an excellent towrope for the dinghy and I fastened it to the outside of the raft to give us a little more space in which to settle down for the night. As evening drew in we had one biscuit and a sip of water, one orange between six, and a glucose sweet each, generally speaking a pretty sumptuous banquet in the light of things to come, but meagre enough rations for us at that time.

Lyn sang 'The Lord Is My Shepherd', and then prayed most earnestly for our safety. As the sun set, the wind grew suddenly colder and we shivered as we drew our terylene sailcloth sheets about us. Lyn suddenly laughed. 'Well, tell us,' we urged. 'When I was swimming to the raft,' she said, 'and it was making that funny noise with the extra gas, Douglas thought the raft was leaking and blocked the pipes with his fingers; he shouted to me to give him a patch; in the middle of the Pacific!' She chuckled again. 'He kept on so I gave him an orange and said, "Will this do?"'

The raft's flotation chambers had gone soft with the cooling of the air, so while Douglas pumped them firm again, Lyn saw to Neil and Robin, both still seasick, and I closed the windward door of the canopy, leaving a peephole for both lookout and ventilation. Robin insisted that he take his share of the adults' two-hour lookout watches in spite of his sickness, and as darkness fell we curled round the boxes and tins, legs and bodies overlapping in places, and tried to rest. The raft was still plunging and lifting in the long fifteen-feet-high swells, while the shorter crested waves, built up under the force of the local winds, surged heavily around us, causing the raft to jerk into the troughs as she brought up sharply on the sea anchor. As we turned and twisted around seeking ease for our aching limbs, we began to experience curious bumps and sharp nudges through the inflated floor of the raft; at first I thought something sharp had wedged under the raft and worried lest it should puncture the flotation chambers, then I heard Lyn give a faint shriek as she too was nudged from below. Douglas, on lookout, said that he could see large fish swimming under the raft, dorado, he thought, and they seemed to be after some smaller fish close under the raft floor.

The bumps and nudges occurred at frequent intervals as the dorado performed their endless gyrations under the raft, often several times in the space of a minute. The severity of the bump depended on the speed and angle of the dorado's impact but generally speaking they were mild compared with the blows from sharks, and quite distinctive from the hard bump of a

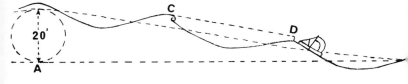

Wav

AB: Swell (caused by distant wind
One every 9 seconds
Height: 20 feet
Length: 300 feet

Swell in this case travels abo

turtle's shell under the floor which we were to experience later. Turtles were also to bite us through the floor of the raft (no doubt an endearing courtship practice) but never hard enough to penetrate the double skin, although they were probably responsible for the leaks which developed in the air chambers of which the raft floor was composed, destroying the buffered effect which the air chambers rendered against the assaults of the fish. There didn't seem to be any shortage of fish around, I thought hopefully; perhaps we wouldn't find it so difficult to supplement our rations after all, but none the less the experience of being poked sharply in the sit-upon when drowsing, or worse, bitten on sit-upon while asleep, was quite startling and we never became accustomed to these assaults during our occupation of the raft.

As we settled down again my mind ranged over the events of the last week for I was trying to remember the distance between the islands in an attempt to arrive at the coordinates for the position in which we had sunk. I knew that our latitude was 1°15′ south of the equator, from the course line on the chart, but I could not remember the longitude of Cape Espinosa although I did remember that Wreck Bay on Chatham Island

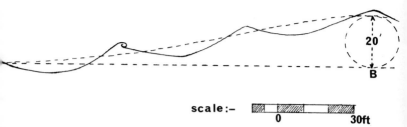

scale:–

0          30ft

CD: Seas (caused by local winds)
    One every 3–4 seconds
    Height: 5–10 feet
    Length: 50 feet

three times faster than Seas

had a longitude of about 89°30'W. If only I'd worked out that dead reckoning position a little sooner, but then, if only a lot of things, and one doesn't normally pay a great deal of attention to terrestrial coordinates when known land is in sight.

Hood Island, I thought, had been roughly on the same longitude as Chatham Island, and we had sailed from there at midnight travelling west by north to Charles Island at about four knots, arriving off Post Office Bay around three in the afternoon, say sixty miles, and had then turned west-north-west to round the south point of Isabela Island the following morning. Allowing for calms and current, I reckoned on a departure of about a hundred and twenty miles before we had turned north for Fernandina Island. My mind came back to the present as the raft floor shuddered under the assault of a dorado and hearing the mumble of voices I turned sideways, lifting on my elbow to see if Robin, taking over the watch from Douglas, was fit enough to keep a good lookout; he fumbled around on the floor of the raft, looking for his glasses, then finding them, leaned out of the raft and vomited emptily at the sea. 'You alright, Robin?' I asked. He muttered something about being as right as you can be when you're stranded on a raft in the middle of the Pacific with no food or water and very seasick; he put his glasses on, 'But if there's a ship about, I'll find it!' He looked at me owlishly in the faint light. 'Let me know if you're in doubt about anything, and don't hesitate to wake me,' I said. I turned on my back again, watching Robin's silhouette moving against the doorway of the canopy as he scanned the horizon; his six-foot frame was thin, but he was tough.

My mind switched back to my longitude calculation. We had stopped at the south end of Fernandina where after an exhausting exploration of the lava beds Neil had been so glad to get back to *Lucette*. 'Good old Lucy' had been home to him.

I glanced over to where Neil lay asleep, his limbs entangled under Sandy's and on top of Lyn's; he was a very loving child, with unorthodox views and a stubborn streak of determination which would stand him in good stead in the days to come. Lyn was worried about his seasickness for his young body would not stand up to the loss of fluid as well as Robin's. Douglas grunted as a dorado collided with the raft under him—'We'll have to do something about these fish, Dad,' he mumbled, half asleep, 'like catching them.'

Doggedly I returned to the problem of longitude. We had made a little easting, say fifteen miles, to travel to the northern side of Fernandina Island then about half that distance west to arrive at Cape Espinosa. So with a departure of a hundred and twelve miles from Wreck Bay the longitude of Espinosa would be roughly 91°20'W.

'Two o'clock!' I jerked awake from my doze to see Robin bending towards me in the darkness. 'Aye aye! Everything alright?' I crawled across to the doorway to take over the watch; the stars twinkled brightly in the arch of darkness beyond the sweep of the sea. Robin gagged at the water; 'No ships,' he muttered and crawled to his place beside Douglas. I peeped round the canopy of the raft at the dinghy; the *Ednamair* lay disconsolately awash at the end of her painter, her white gunwhale just visible above the surface of the water. She was helping the sea anchor, I supposed, but we'd have to bail her out first thing in the morning, for the wooden thwarts, which contained the polystyrene flotation reserve, would loosen and come adrift if they became waterlogged.

The water exploded as a thirty-pound dorado leapt high in

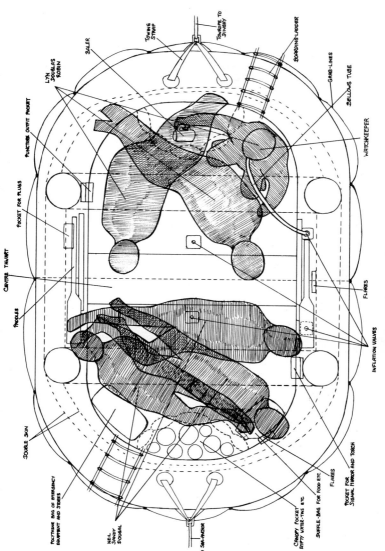

Usual disposition of bodies in raft at night

the air after a flying fish, landing with a slap on its side in
a shower of luminescence. I glanced down to where several
large fish swam under the raft, constantly rising to skim the
underside of the raft's edge, sometimes hitting it a heavy blow
with their high jutting foreheads. Douglas was right, we should
have to do something about these fish!

### Second day

The long night paled into the beautiful dawn sky of the South
Pacific; slowly we collected our scattered wits for already our
dreams of being elsewhere than on the raft had taken on the
vivid reality of hallucination. Wretched with cramp and discomfort it had been such a simple solution to go next door and
there I would find my childhood bed, so clear in every forgotten
detail, waiting for me.

The pressure in the raft's flotation chambers had dropped
drastically during the night so our first task was to top up with
air. We connected the bellows pipe to the non-return valve and
started pumping, taking turns to keep the bellows going; after
fifteen minutes we could see no improvement in the pressure so
we disconnected the bellows and tested them for leaks; there
weren't any bad ones, but the air intake didn't close properly
and most of the air escaped the way it went in. Douglas and I
looked at each other; we knew the answer to this one for the
bellows we had used for our old inflatable dinghy had similarly
served us. We cut the pipe from the bellows, not without
difficulty, for the curve of the knife prevented any sawing action,
then placing the pipe in his mouth Douglas blew mightily. We
took turn about for a few minutes and the raft was soon back
to normal, but we knew even then that we had not seen the last
of this particular trouble.

I looked across at Lyn, rubbing the cramp out of the twins'
legs. 'We'll see to the *Ednamair* after breakfast'; I looked hopefully at the water jar, but it was nearly empty. We had emptied
the glucose sweets out of their glass jar so that it could be used
to hold drinking water as it was decanted from the tin, for
although we had discussed the issue of equal rations of water
(there wasn't enough to do that) we had decided simply to pass
the jar round, each person limiting him or herself to the

minimum needed to carry on; at the same time, the visible water level in the jar enabled everyone to see there was no cheating. Breakfast consisted of one quarter-ounce biscuit, a piece of onion and a sip of water, except for Robin and Neil who could not eat and were with difficulty persuaded to take some extra water with a seasick pill. We had used two pints of water in one day between six, hardly a maintenance ration under a tropic sun, which I remembered had been placed as high as two pints per person per day! We ate slowly, savouring each taste of onion and biscuit with a new appreciation and, although we hardly felt as if we had breakfasted on bacon and eggs, we were still sufficiently shocked at our altered circumstances not to feel hunger.

Breakfast over, Lyn, with Sandy helping, sorted out the various pieces of sail which were to be used for bedding, chatting quietly all the while to Neil and Robin. Douglas and I went to the door of the raft and, pulling the dinghy alongside, first attempted to bail it out as it lay swamped, but the waves filled it as fast as we bailed. We turned its stern towards us and, lifting slowly, allowed the bow to submerge, then when we could lift it no higher, I called 'Let go!' The dinghy flopped back in the water with three inches of freeboard, we bailed desperately with small bailers, then Douglas took one of the wooden boxes and with massive scoops bailed enough water out to allow him to board the dinghy and bail it dry. We were all cheered by the sight of little *Ednamair* afloat again, and with a cry of delight Douglas held up his Timex watch; it had been lying in the bottom of the dinghy all this time and was still going! He also found what was to prove our most valuable possession, the stainless-steel kitchen knife which I had thrown in after the fruit.

After a segment of orange each for elevenses we loaded the oars, a paddle, the empty boxes, the petrol can, the hundred-foot raft painter, and the piece of the genoa designated for the dinghy sail, then climbing into the dinghy started work on the jury rig that was to turn the *Ednamair* into a tugboat for our first stage of the journey north. Douglas, in the meantime, helped Lyn to reorganise the inside of the raft now that there was much more room, and topped up the flotation chambers with air.

I rigged one oar in the mast step with appropriate fore and

back stays (I had rigged *Ednamair* as a sailing dinghy in Colon, but leeboards, mast and sail had been stowed below in *Lucette* for the ocean passage and had of course been lost), then cutting notches in the raft paddle, bent the head of the sail on to it to form a square sail. I had previously taken the precaution of making the luff wire, shackled to the towing straps of the raft, fast to the ringbolt in the bow of the dinghy, in case the nylon painter had frayed. I had decided the dinghy would have to perform her function of towing by proceeding stern first, for her cutaway stern could not be exposed to the overtaking waves without danger of swamping. The paddle was made fast to the top of the oar, and the sail foot secured to the two ends of the other oar, placed athwartships across the rowlock sockets. A violent jerk sent me sprawling into the bottom of the boat and I realised that we were operational.

I climbed back aboard the raft for a lunch of a small piece of fortified bread, of which there was about a pound and a half in the emergency rations along with eight ounces of glucose, and a mouthful of water; I felt very thirsty after my exertions in the dinghy. *Ednamair* was now straining at the leash so I called to Douglas to trip the sea anchor and haul it aboard; the time was two o'clock in the afternoon and we had started our voyage to the Doldrums, and, I shuddered at the thought of the alternative, rain. I estimated our position at Latitude 1° South and Longitude 94°40′ West or, more accurately, two hundred miles west of Cape Espinosa.

The white plastic-covered luff wire was now snapping taut with considerable force as *Ednamair* yawed at the end of her towrope, so having little use for the petrol I lashed the can to the centre of the towing wire to act as a tension buffer which it did quite effectively. We now turned our attention to the flotation chambers of the raft to see if we could find any leaks. The raft, an old model, had been a gift from our friend Captain Siggi Thorsteinsson of the Icelandic rescue craft *Bonnie*; Siggi with his wife Etta and their family had run parallel to our voyage on *Lucette* from Falmouth to Miami; we remembered, with deep gratitude, his concern when our previous inflatable had become such a doubtful asset that he had presented us with one of the two which they carried. I had expressed my hope at the time that we would never find occasion to use it, thanked him warmly for it, cursed its unwieldy bulk many a time on our cramped coach roof and felt comforted by its presence thereon, nevertheless. Now? Well, you never can tell, but we probably owed our lives to it. The double canopy alone was worth a gallon of water a day to us in keeping out the heat of the sun, and its emergency rations were available to us now only because they were already stowed inside the raft.

We examined the raft's flotation chambers as well as we could, pouring water over all the exposed surface areas, but could find no leaks, although there were one or two repair patches, and finally put down the loss of air to seepage through the treated fabric of the raft. We arranged a regular routine of topping up on each watch to keep the raft as rigid as possible, for the continuous flexing of the softened chambers by the waves was bound to cause wear. The double floor in the after section of the raft, which was divided by a central flotation piece, had been holed from below and a tiny hole in the upper skin was allowing the sea water to seep through to our bedding and required us to perform mopping up operations at fairly frequent intervals. We tried to repair the leak with sticking plaster but with no success. The sun now dipping towards the horizon, our attention was turned to other things which had to be checked before nightfall. The lashings on the towing wire, the sail and the rigging on the dinghy were inspected and made secure where they looked in need of attention. I tripped the two small drogues at the forward end of the raft to increase our speed which I estimated to be about one knot, plus a set from the current of one knot, all in a nor' nor' westerly direction.

We gathered round for 'tea', and our meal of a one and a half square inch biscuit each, a small piece of glucose and a mouthful of water was shared by all, Neil and Robin having regained their sea legs with the help of the pills. As dusk drew in, Lyn settled the twins to sleep after playing 'I spy', and singing to them. Robin was more cheerful and chatted about his travels across the continent of America by bus, working casually for his keep, and as we listened, we wondered if we would ever see land again. During the day Lyn had cut pieces of sail for the twins and Douglas to write letters, telling their friends in England and America what had happened, while she had written a loving farewell letter to our nineteen-year-old

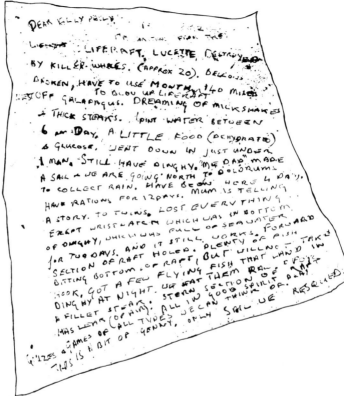

Letter written by Douglas on a piece of genoa sail.
*Above*—Front. *Opposite*—Back.

daughter Anne who had left us in the Bahamas to follow her own destiny. Robin had written to his mother, and I added a footnote to Anne's letter sending her my best wishes for her happiness in life with my love. In the footnote to Robin's I apologised for having been instrumental in bringing his life to such an untimely end. These farewell notes were placed in a waterproof wrapping and tucked in one of the pockets of the raft, for we knew that when the time came to write such farewell

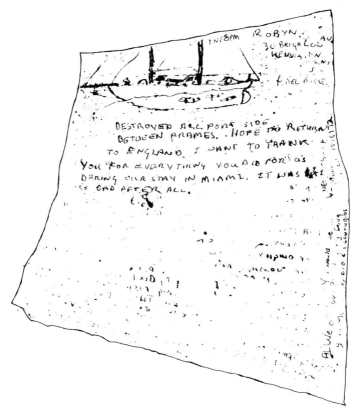

letters, we would be unable, both in mind and body, to cope
with the effort. We all felt a little sad and depressed at the
prospect of our imminent demise especially Neil, who, I felt,
could visualise more clearly the privations which lay ahead of
us without knowing the possibilities of the ways in which they
could be avoided. He had looked a very sad and forlorn little
boy, lying in his mother's arms gazing, unblinking, into space
and seeing heaven knows what terrors in his mind's eye, but

Neil's logbook, written on a piece of raft canopy

now tucked in beside Sandy under sheets of sail cloth, chatted quietly about friends in Miami and Colon.

Robin had first watch tonight and I warned him which points needed watching on the dinghy which, in the increasing wind, was pulling hard on the towrope and yawing widely as the pull on her sail swung the stern around. (The dinghy, as explained, was proceeding stern first to permit her to ride the seas without swamping.) As I settled down beside Lyn she leaned across and whispered, close to tears, 'If Neil "goes" I shall not allow him to go alone.' I felt shocked that she could even be thinking in terms of death, even though we had just completed our farewell letters 'in case'. I put my hand out and clasped hers; 'I don't think it will come to that,' I said steadily,

'but if it did, you could help more by staying.' Lyn was one of
the most competent people I have ever met to have helping in
an emergency, and my deep respect for her capabilities as a
nurse and as a wife and mother had grown steadily over our
twenty years of married life. I feared that she was holding back
on something in Neil's medical condition that I did not know
of, to make her so despondent, but as she talked it became clear
to me that the shock of the last thirty-six hours was catching up
on her, as it had with me, so I talked of our chances of being
picked up and if we weren't, of the possibility of reaching the
coast of Central America, maintaining ourselves on fish which
I felt we could catch, and rain water to drink. 'And the rain
our drink,' she murmured (Han Suyin had worked for a while
as a doctor in the Hong Kong hospital where Lyn had been
sister) and I knew she was no longer thinking of death, or for
that matter of Malaya, but of the happy days we had spent
sailing together in Hong Kong where we were married. 'I'll
draw you a map tomorrow,' I said, wriggling around to find a
comfortable place for my head; there wasn't one. Neil's and
Sandy's legs were crossed over the top of my body and I could
feel the pool of sea water, which had seeped through the hole
in the floor, gathering under my bottom. 'Pass me the sponge
and the bailer,' I muttered to Lyn, as she got ready to go on
watch, and silently she passed them to me, our hands touching
and understanding in the darkness. Dry underneath again, I
lay down to think in the long hours of the night of how long it
would take us to reach the Doldrums and of our chances of
finding rain there; an exercise that was to occupy my nights with
increasing urgency as our meagre store of water cans gradually
dwindled. Robin had puffed rather ineffectually at the inflating
tube before he went off watch, but the raft was still pretty soft,
so I stuck the end in my mouth and gave it a good blow at both
ends; Robin would get better at it as he got used to the idea.

### Third day

My watch, in the dawn hours of the morning, started with a
clear sky, but, as the sun tinted the clouds, the wind freshened
again from the south and the tall flowery cumulus, pink peaked
with grey bases, seemed heavy enough to give rain. As soon as

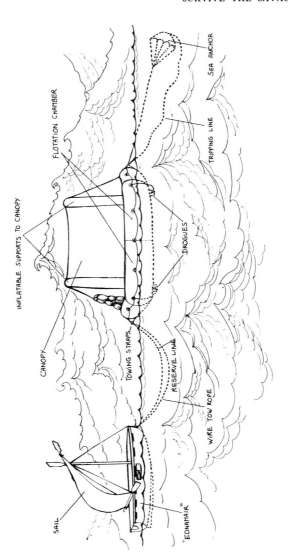

*Ednamair* towing raft with sea anchor streamed

it was light I pulled in the dinghy and climbed aboard to inspect
the sail fastenings and stays, one of which had worked loose in
the night. While I was securing the stay I caught sight of a
small black shape under the wooden box by the thwart; I
stooped and lifted our first contribution from the sea, a flying
fish of about eight inches. I gutted and descaled it, then passed
it over to Lyn, now awake, for her to marinate it in a squeeze
of lemon juice, which acted as a cooking agent. We breakfasted
at seven, an hour later, each savouring our tiny piece of fish
done to a turn in the lemon juice, followed by a crunchy piece
of onion and a mouthful of water. The raft had begun pitching
heavily again, surging on the crests of the breaking sea and
dropping steeply into the troughs. To our disappointment, both
Neil and Robin started being seasick again and though we
offered them seasick pills they decided to do without and try to
get used to the motion of the raft instead.

The waves began to break over the stern of the raft, and with
swells of up to twenty feet high, it looked as if we were in for a
bad day. *Ednamair* yawed violently as the wind gusted in her
sail and she pulled hard on the towrope, lifting it clear of the
water at times. I decided to take a reef in the sail to ease the
strain on the towing straps of the raft, so Douglas hauled the
dinghy alongside the raft and held her while I balanced precariously on the seat. To reef her, I simply tied a rope around the
belly of the sail, giving it an hour-glass effect and reducing its
effective pulling power by half. I had just completed the
operation and was standing up again to return when a large
breaker surged round the raft and caught the dinghy broadside.
As she tilted, I lost balance and fell, grabbing at the mast to
prevent myself falling into the sea; *Ednamair* tilted sharply with
the increased leverage and the sea rushed in over the gunwhale
in a wave. Before I could let go the mast and drop to the floor
of the dinghy, it was swamped. Luckily we retained about three
inches of freeboard and before the next wave could complete
the damage, I dived through the door of the canopy into the
raft, and the dinghy, relieved of my weight, floated a little
higher. We bailed desperately for several minutes from the raft
and then, gaining on the influx of water slopping over the gunwhale, we finally got enough freeboard to allow me to return to
the *Ednamair* and bail it dry again. In the night, I had thought

of the possibility of us taking to the dinghy altogether and leaving the raft, but this incident served to highlight the difficulty of any such move; the subject of trim with a very small freeboard would be of paramount importance and now I doubted if the dinghy could take the six of us and remain afloat in the open sea.

After our exhausting morning, we rested awhile, lunching on a mouthful of water and a few 'crumbs' of a type of fortified bread which, although made up in tablet form, disintegrated at the first touch and made the conveyance of the crumbs from container to mouth an operation that required great care to avoid spilling and usually resulted in some waste, even when we licked the stray crumbs off our clothes. This was followed by a piece of orange.

The clouds thickened as the day advanced and the high cumulus began to drop rain in isolated showers. The wind freshened still further and with the surf of breaking waves slopping through the canopy door at the rear of the raft, we closed the drawstrings on the flaps as much as was possible without cutting off all ventilation. With the large blanket pin I punched bigger holes in the empty water cans and made plugs to fit them in case a shower should cross us and give us water, while Douglas blew lustily into the pipe to make the raft as rigid as possible in the heavy seas. *Ednamair* bounced around at the end of her towrope like a pup on a leash and I was considering taking the sail down altogether when the patter of raindrops on the canopy warned us that we were about to get rain. A pipe led down from the centre of the rain catchment area on the roof and, pulling this to form a depression in the roof, we prepared to gather our first rainwater. With fascinated eyes we gazed at the mouth of the pipe, at the liquid that dribbled from the end, bright yellow, and saltier than the sea. As soon as the salt had been washed off the roof, we managed to collect half a pint of yellowish rubbery-tasting liquid before the shower passed over. I looked at the jar of fluid (one could hardly call it water) sadly; we would need to do a lot better than that if we were to survive.

The raft, now pitching heavily, required blowing up every hour to keep it rigid, and the undulations and jerks did nothing to ease the spasms of seasickness which Neil and Robin were suffering; they both looked drawn and pale, refusing even water in spite of Lyn's pleading. As the raft slid up the twenty-foot swells to the breaking combers at the top, Lyn prayed desperately for calm weather and for rain, urging that the rest of us should join her in prayer with such insistence that I had to remind her that freedom of thought and religion was a matter of individual choice and no one should be coerced. Lyn looked at me, startled, and continued praying aloud while Robin, on the verge of making a facetious remark, stilled his tongue with it half said; although he described himself as a non-practising Christian the religious fervour with which Lyn had appealed to us embarrassed him. Silence, interrupted only by the hiss and roar of the breaking waves, followed Lyn's praying, then quietly she sang 'The Lord Is My Shepherd' to the twins as I put away the still empty cans and the jar containing the foul-tasting yellow stuff; it was better than sea water.

I passed the water jar around for 'sippers' before our meagre ration of biscuit, reminding everyone that our supplies were now very low and that only minimal amounts should be taken. 'We must try to drink less than two pints per day between us,' I said, 'We have only twelve tins left and we still have over three hundred miles to go.' A quart of water each for the next three hundred miles, it didn't sound much.

As darkness closed in and the first watchkeeper settled to his two-hour vigil, I could feel the bump and bite of the dorado fish through the bottom of the raft and resolved to try to catch one in the morning. Neil and Sandy were sleeping soundly after helping to blow up the raft and mop up the water which was now coming through the floor at a greater rate than before. They looked so vulnerable that my heart turned over at the prospect of what lay ahead for them; death by thirst, or starvation, or just a slow deterioration into exhaustion. I heard Lyn's voice many times that night, in my mind: 'We must get these boys to land,' and sleep would not come to ease the burden of my conscience.

### Fourth day

During the night the wind fell to a gentle breeze and seas calmed to tolerable conditions which allowed the raft to move easily in the seaway. Dawn brought a clear sky and the promise

of a hot day, but at least the calmer weather would allow Neil
and Robin to make a recovery from their seasickness. The cry
of 'Pissoir' for the bailing jar, which we used for urinating in,
to avoid the necessity of the persons relieving themselves to get
to the doorway over sleeping bodies, was heard less often now
and our urine had taken on a very dark colour. I·had contem-
plated tasting some to find out if it was at all palatable but Lyn
said that she had already tried hers. 'It was very salty,' she said
rather sadly. 'I understand from an article I once read by some
Professor that we might derive some benefit from drinking each
other's.' 'Would you like to try some of mine?' I said. We both
burst out laughing; 'Not yet, thanks.' Douglas looked at us
disgustedly from the doorway. 'For God's sake!' he said,
'What's for breakfast?'

Flying Fish

I climbed over to *Ednamair* to shake the reef out of the sail,
and to my delight found a large and a small flying fish in the
bottom of the boat. They were duly dressed, then divided with
much ceremony, and the heads saved for bait. Robin and Neil
looked better now and were able to eat their share with a little
extra water. I watched Lyn carefully to see that she took her sip
of water, and when she didn't, insisted that she should do so,
for we could not afford to have her sick, anyway not that way;
if we were going to die from dehydration, we'd do it together.
We chewed our piece of onion and segment of orange slowly,
doing without the biscuit this morning, for the dry food was
going too quickly. 'We shall have to try to catch some fish,' I

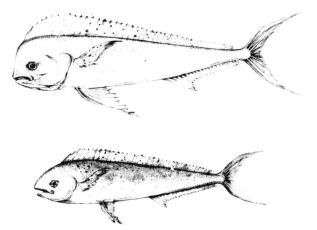

Dorado: male (with high forehead) and female

said. 'We put the line out yesterday morning,' Lyn called, 'when you were working with the dinghy, but when we pulled it in the hook had gone.' She looked across at Sandy—'Did you try again?' Sandy shook his head. 'No bait, we only had one fish head.' He looked questioningly at me and I wondered what could have taken the hook (probably a shark in view of the absence of any struggle) but said nothing. 'I'll try the spinner from the dinghy; if that doesn't work we'll try some more bait.'

I climbed back into *Ednamair* to try my hand at catching a dorado. Since they are game fish and feed mostly on flying fish, I would either have to use live bait or a spinner, and since I had a spinner I decided to try that. I looked doubtfully at the wire trace, wondering if it would be strong enough, then fixing some weights to it, ran out a length of line. Before casting I took a couple of turns around the mast with the line and then, swinging the spinner, cast it thirty feet to the lee side, pulling in smartly to make the spinner travel. To my surprise three dorado dashed for the spinner, but turned away before striking; they were big fish and would surely break the line if I did catch one. I looked around, perhaps I could cast at a smaller one. I stretched out more line and made a few tentative casts in the direction of

some smaller fish, rather like small jacks, but they ignored the
flash of the spinner though once again the big dorado followed
but did not strike. Three small female dorado suddenly swam
near, and excited, I cast the spinner well out and ahead of them.
To my utter dismay I watched the spool curve outwards in a
gentle arc after the spinner, land in the water and sink quietly
into the depths. The line had gone. I was tempted to go after it
but a lively deterrent in the shape of a large triangular fin
belonging to a white-tipped shark appeared on the other side of
the raft and I cursed my stupidity in frustrated anguish. How
could I have been so careless as to leave the line unfastened to
the mast? Our only spinner and our only wire trace, chucked
over the side as if I were a kid at a Sunday school picnic. My
knuckles beat at my brow; if I was going to make stupid mistakes
like this now, what would it be like later? This was the sort of
carelessness that cost lives at sea and if I was making these
mistakes now what could I reasonably expect from newcomers
to the sea like Robin, or youngsters like Neil and Sandy? I
resolved to examine every move before I made it, and every
decision before we acted upon it, for sooner or later, because I
had overlooked something, someone would die.

I made my apologies to the others for losing the line and set
to work immediately, made another spinner from the tinfoil
on the lid of the 'crumbs box', attached hook and weight to the
nylon line and was ready to cast again by midday. The twins
had spruced up with Mum's help and had actually combed
their hair, they looked ready to go ashore! Returning to the
dinghy, I cast in all directions for nearly an hour, trolling at
different speeds, trying variations of red and white bunting on
the spinner and flying fish heads on the hook, but all to no avail,
the dorado would follow the line with interest but would not
strike. I gave up, exhausted, my mouth dry with thirst under the
noonday sun, and tumbled back into the raft, depressed but
glad to be in the cool again. Douglas, on watch for ships,
motioned me to the door of the raft and pointed to the sinister
triangular fin approaching and we gazed in dumb awe as the
ten-foot long torpedo-shaped shark glided quietly under the
raft, its attendant bevy of pilot fish in perfect arrowhead
formation across its back. We looked at each other and made a
silent pact not to tell the twins of our unwelcome company.

Lunch, consisting of a piece of orange (we now ate the peel as well) and a half biscuit, followed by a small mouthful of water, was over all too soon and we settled down in the afternoon to rest during the heat of the day. The twins were finishing a sketch of '*Lucette* and the whales' with pencil on sailcloth and Lyn was embroidering a message on some blue cotton in case our written letters were obliterated by immersion in sea water. It seemed a good time to draw my chart, so I fetched a piece of wood from the dinghy as a table and taking a dried-out chart reference map which we had saved from the now pulped *West Indies Pilot*, marked in the coordinates from the Panama Canal to the Marquesas Islands, with the Galapagos, and as many of the islands as I could remember to the north. I then drew in the rhumb line route from the Marquesas to the Canal and our own position and projected route to the Doldrums. 'We should start crossing our next possible shipping route in a couple of days' time,' I remarked. Robin leaned over and studied my tiny squiggles of positions. 'How far to land?' he queried. 'I'll have to draw that on a different scale,' I said, 'but you can see from this that if we don't see anything on the route from the Canal westwards our next chance won't come until we cross the route from North America to Peru or Chile and we'll have to get east of the Galapagos for that.'

I marked out a larger scale and drew in the square from the American coast through the Galapagos to the position where we were sunk then northwards to take in the whole of the Doldrums area, which at this time of the year stretched from about 5°N to 15°N, spreading out at each limit to about 20° of latitude as it neared the Central American coast. Then, more difficult, I lightly pencilled in the route which I thought we might take for the coast, north-west to the Doldrums, then east-by-north or north-easterly to the coast. I had difficulty remembering which country started where on that stretch of coastline but I knew it ran in a north-westerly direction all the way to Mexico, and Robin although he had travelled down the isthmus by bus, was unable to help me much, but he could see that we would land several hundred miles north of Panama, 'Perhaps around Nicaragua,' he thought. I drew in our position, on the larger scale chart, which I now estimated to be about 1°30′ North and 220 miles west of Espinosa (about 95°W) and measured our distance from the Doldrums limit. 'About two hundred and fifty miles to go before we get rain,' I murmured, 'two hundred and fifty miles at fifty miles a day, five days and we have'—I looked over to where the cans of water lay on the raft floor—'ten tins of water left, we'll just make it.'

I tried to sound cheerful and, while we could see that we had already grown thinner, we weren't exactly emaciated; indeed, although Neil and Robin could ill afford to lose any weight from their already thin frames, I had been putting on weight before the disaster, Sandy and Douglas were well fleshed, and Lyn had a pound or two of fat which she could afford to lose. We had good body reserves to live on if only we could reach the rain area and if the wind held, but that was the rub, the wind would die away before we reached the Doldrums, so would the north-westerly current, and our margin for error was lamentably small, how long we would drift between trade winds and the rain area was anybody's guess. Robin looked at my little map and pointed questioningly to some squiggly arrows I had drawn on it. 'Those represent the counter current which runs through the Doldrums, and when we get into that we'll be getting a lift in the right direction. I don't think I've seen an estimate of the drift of the counter current, but it should be half a knot anyway.' I hoped it would be more, but it would be a bad blow to our morale if at the end of many weeks of agonising struggle we did not find land when we expected it. I measured up the distance in the curved courseline I expected us to take, with a can opener—'About a thousand miles, fifty days at twenty miles a day; it doesn't sound bad if you say it quickly.' If we already looked thin after four days, I thought, what sort of condition would we be in after fifty? It was a grim prospect. 'Of course, we could reasonably expect to be picked up before then,' I said confidently. 'If nowhere else then most certainly on the busy coastal shipping routes to the Panama Canal.' Robin now looked a bit more cheerful, and he chatted happily to Lyn about his experiences as a porter in various hotels in Wales and Ireland during the university holidays. I had said nothing of the tiny islands, one, perhaps two, which lay between us and the mainland; it would be nice if we could land on one of them, but that would be a matter of luck, not navigation.

The raft now required topping up with air at much shorter

intervals, three or four times a watch, and though we looked
again for a leak, it wasn't until Lyn went on watch in the
evening that she spotted the tell-tale bubbles rising from under
the towing straps. We spread out the puncture outfit to see if
we could use any of the patches with the remains of the rubber
solution, which had a consistency of chewing gum. The patches
were old ones too, and didn't have the sealing compound on
them which one finds in a good modern outfit. We had four
rubber plugs, some patches of ordinary rubberised fabric, and
a bit of emery paper. We would have to try something in the
morning.

9-foot White-tipped Shark, one of our constant companions

As the evening drew in and we had supped our morsels of
food and water, we were talking about ways in which we might
catch the dorado. I had said that, if we plunged our hands downwards as they skimmed under the edge of the raft, there was
bound to come a time when we could grip them where the body
of the fish narrows to the tail, the only place where it is possible
to grasp and hold the slippery, streamlined body of the dorado.
We might have to try hundreds of times but, since we had
nothing else to do at night except look for ships and blow up the
raft, we could try in our spare moments. Sandy's voice piped
up as he asked casually if nobody else had seen the sharks
around; he'd just seen another two, and he'd wondered if they

were the big fish we'd been talking about to Mum. 'They're maneaters too!' he said interestedly. We looked at each other and laughed at our secrecy when we found out that Neil and Sandy had been talking about them all evening. It would take more than a rotten old shark to frighten them.

During the night watch Lyn told me how she could sometimes see her sisters Edna and Mary, after whom the dinghy was named, in the dinghy pulling us towards safety and she often talked with them in the long lonely hours of watchkeeping. (Lyn often took an extra watch to allow Douglas or Robin a little more sleep.) That night, however, the task of topping up became an exhausting fifteen-minute interval marathon, the forward flotation chambers losing pressure rapidly as soon as we stopped blowing.

### Fifth day

Dawn brought a beautiful sunrise. The sea, now quiet in the gentle southerly breeze, reflected the beautiful colours of the Pacific with incredibly intense blues and reds ranging into delicate tints of green and pink, the whole sky a blaze of glorious colour.

Another two flying fish this morning, one from the dinghy, the other had flown through the door of the raft during Robin's watch with so much flap and slap it sounded like a twenty-pound fish. These provided us with breakfast of a two-inch strip of fish each. Pacific flying fish are much smaller than their Atlantic brethren, and in the Galapagos area the number of predators which live on flying fish, amongst other things, gives one occasion to marvel at the fact that there are any left at all.

After breakfast we allowed the raft to deflate at the towing end, where we had located the leak under the towing strap at about three inches below the water line. Then with Douglas holding the strain of the dinghy on the towrope, we doubled the floor back and managed to bring the damaged area into the raft. Three small holes leaked air in an area of torn fabric under the strap (*Ednamair*'s pull on the towrope had been too vigorous in the strong breeze). The surface was cleaned and allowed to dry in the hot sunshine, then after roughening the surface with the emery paper I tried to get the dried-out solution to stick in and around the small holes, with no success.

We decided to try varnish; the coats of varnish took half an hour to become tacky in the strong sun, and after applying three coats to the raft and the patches, we stuck them together and waited a further hour for the varnish to harden, but not so that it was brittle. Blown up, the raft deflated even more quickly than before, and puzzled, I lifted the towing straps clear again. The patches seemed alright. I called to Robin to inflate the damaged area again while I held it up and as the pressure built up the hiss of escaping air came from further along the side of the flotation chamber. I leaned over the doubled-up raft and found the hole, a quarter of an inch in diameter, worn in the fabric by one of the drogue trip ropes. No wonder we'd had to keep blowing! I plugged this one with a rubber stopper, and lashed the paper-thin fabric tight around the plug with nylon thread, then noting that the varnished patches had started peeling off, I stripped them off altogether, enlarged the pinholes in the fabric enough to insert rubber plugs in them and we blew up the chamber again, turn about, sitting in a row like the three wise monkeys. It stayed up this time and we relaxed, happily relieved of our blowing routine for a while anyway. Robin's blowing prowess was growing by leaps and bounds, and he was filling his lungs and blowing with great gusto, improving his technique daily. I felt the exercise must be doing him a lot of good!

During the afternoon we played Twenty Questions; Neil was particularly good at guessing the object, especially when Sandy had chosen it, before many questions had been asked, whereas Robin was masterful at tracking down the objective with shrewd questions. I worked out our noon position at 2°06′ North, 230 miles west of Espinosa (I had decided to stick to a longitude relative to the Galapagos for it saved explaining our position in terms of land) and announced that we were now entering an area in which there just might be a ship. (Robin had worked out that there should be one passing through the area every two days if twenty-five per cent of the French and New Zealand traffic took the Rhumb line route north of Galapagos, but his basis of information came from my guesswork which was none too knowledgeable in shipping volumes.) Cumulus cloud built up again during the day but the only visible shower of rain falling from the base of the cloud in a grey curtain missed us by miles. I wondered if Robin would be interested in a statistical exercise of shower probability but he declined on the grounds that he would have to be supplied with necessary data over a period of years. I made a mental note that statistics, unless based on local data, was a dead duck, and that a theoretical education could only supply a man with a theoretical living, the thirst that we suffered at that moment being anything but theoretical.

The rain came just after dark, a heavy shower of short duration from which we collected half a pint of brackish yellow rubber-smelling water, and a pint of ordinary yellow rubber-smelling water in that order. As our excitement subsided with the passing of the shower, we settled down again in our now continuously wet clothing, though hardly to sleep, for I rarely slept at all now, listening all the time to the sounds of the raft, the sea, the fish, the dinghy, and thinking of ways of catching fish, of the possibility of straining plankton from the sea, and of covering the raft canopy with sailcloth to exclude the filthy yellow dye from the water; of what would happen to us when the raft became untenable as it would do in time to come. I knew that Lyn too lay awake at night, and that her thoughts were never far away from methods of getting food and water into the twins' bodies, and of helping them and us to survive in this alien environment. We now welcomed our call to go on watch, if only to relieve the burden of our minds in action, and to stop having to pretend to rest.

At about ten o'clock a strange new sound like a giant breath exhaled intruded on the usual noises; we listened with bated breath as it came closer. Douglas, on watch, grunted from the door of the raft 'Whale'. This time Lyn and the children were frightened (I was none too happy myself!) for the memory of the killer whales had grown more terrible with the passing of time and their fear that the raft would now be attacked was shared in some degree by us all. We soon identified it as a large, slow-moving Sei whale, one of the types that is preyed upon by the killers, and though I tried to reassure Lyn that this one would not harm us for it lives by straining tiny plankton organisms from the sea, she prayed with desperate appeal that we be spared a second attack. The whale surfaced many times around us during the following thirty minutes, often coming

50-foot Sei Whale

quite close. Sandy had fallen asleep again and now the whale's blowing coincided so accurately with Sandy's snoring that we all ended up laughing at the duet.

A water leak developed in the forward compartment of the raft later in the night although the buoyancy compartment in the floor seemed undamaged; the influx of water seemed to come from the area where the dorado struck the raft most, between floor and side compartments, and made for more discomfort in the already trying circumstances. The after flotation compartment had started going soft for no apparent reason and I resolved to look for more leaks in the morning.

### Sixth day

This day started, apart from watch-keeping, at the early hour of two in the morning when a noise like a sail in a gale, flapping and a-slapping, from *Ednamair* announced that a large fish had miscalculated its flight path and was trying to put the error to rights.

Quickly pulling the dinghy alongside the raft I jumped aboard and fell on top of the huge dorado struggling in the bottom of the boat, its body arching violently in its attempts to escape. Hanging on with one hand to the part just forward of the tail, I pulled the knife from the thwart where it was kept, plunged it into the head just behind the eye, and sawed desperately, finally severing the head altogether, then just to make sure that no reflex action would reactivate it, I cut its tail off as well. It was a beautiful thirty-five pounder and I quickly informed everyone within hearing distance of the joyful news, and washing the blood from my hands, chest and legs as best as I could in the darkness, returned to the raft to wait for daylight. At four in the morning we were dozing quietly when a flying fish flew straight through the door of the raft, striking Lyn in the face. Now Lyn is a very steady and reliable person in a crisis, she seems to be able to do the right thing at the right time automatically while less able people like myself are floundering around wondering what to do, but her reaction to being slapped in the face by a wet fish at four in the morning, after all our previous excitement, had us all scrambling around the raft looking for something like the Loch Ness monster until the eight-inch leviathan was finally secured and made safe for breakfast.

There was no sleep for us after that and as soon as daylight had dispelled the shadows inside the raft, I returned to the *Ednamair* to dress the dorado; I saved the liver and heart for breakfast along with the huge backbone, the head, and some thicker pieces of soft white fleshed fillet from the back. The rest I cut into long strips and hung from the stays to dry in the sun. Our larder was off to a flying start in more ways than one! While cleaning the boat out I found another flying fish lying in the bottom under the sail and so we had our first decent breakfast since *Lucette* had been so roughly taken from us. Fish, flavoured with lemon juice and onion, and a concoction of fish liver and heart with small pieces of flying fish also marinated in lemon juice, followed by our last orange (it was going bad) and a sip of water. Our stomachs, unaccustomed to this bulk, felt quite full, and afterwards as we lay down to digest this huge meal, we picked at a section of backbone each, Robin gnawing at the head in good old-fashioned caveman style, while the rest of us first picked the bone clean then, under Lyn's direction, split the vertebrae to find the spinal fluid, full of protein and fresh water. Even Neil, who seemed to find his hunger more irksome than the rest of us, declared himself content.

I had the heads of two flying fish and some offal from the dead fish at my disposal so I went over to the *Ednamair* after

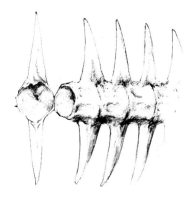

Fluid can be sucked from the spinal cavities of a fish

breakfast with the fishing line and some hooks, determined to have another go at the dorado. I tried a large hook first, casting well out from the dinghy to try to avoid the bait being eaten by the small scavenger fish which surrounded us, but as I trolled the bait in towards the dinghy, the scavenger fish were on to it in a flash, their small mouths and sharp teeth making a mockery of the large hook, and tearing the bait from it. The dorado, although they followed the bait, made no attempt to strike, so I weighted the line with a sinker and after baiting the hook again, sent it fifty feet deep, avoiding the scavenger fish by casting well out. Tensely I waited for the strike, and when it came after fifteen minutes I wasn't ready for it—an almost gentle pull, then nothing; slowly I pulled in the bare end of line, hook and sinker gone. Shark's teeth are razor sharp and make short work even of a steel trace at times; they cut through my nylon line like butter.

I fixed a small hook on the end of the line, baited it with offal and tried to catch the scavengers, but my smallest hook was far too big to fit into their mouths and they merely ate the bait off the hook as fast as I put it on. By midday I was tired of feeding the fish and returned to the raft with the lumps of dorado for lunch (I felt we ought to eat the wet fish while it was available for we wouldn't be able to eat it after it was dry until we had enough water to drink with it). I put our

noon position at 2°40′ North and 240 miles west of Espinosa;
no ships, no rain, but there was a trace of cirrus stratus cloud
in the northern sky, forerunner of weather systems and of
storms. Douglas and Robin were busy investigating the influx
of water into the forward compartment of the raft, and found
the seepage to be coming through a paper-thin section of fabric
between the bottom and the side flotation chambers; Lyn had
found another small hole in the floor of the after section, which
we were able to plug with a small piece of rubber, and Douglas
had located the air leak in the after port-side flotation chamber,
well under the water and impossible to investigate without
lifting the raft out of the water completely, or turning it upside
down.

The sky darkened from the north as the afternoon progressed
and I looked hopefully for signs of rain, but the gentle layer of
strato-cumulus showed unmistakable signs of an occluded front,
no longer active, no rain; but we took heart from the simple
fact of its presence, for it was travelling south above the trade
winds, coming from the Doldrums, and with only seven pints
of water left, we needed an encouraging sign of some sort. The
cloud belt had sheltered us from the heat of the sun during the
early hours of the afternoon, but now as the skies cleared, the
radiated heat of the declining sun beat into the raft and we
lapsed into silent endurance until evening, occasionally splashing water on what was left of our clothes and on the raft, to
reduce raft and body heat. Our clothing had suffered wear and
tear from early on, and Douglas had now discarded his tattered
swimming trunks completely to ease the pain from the area of
raw flesh around his buttocks and thighs, developed through
continuous contact with the salt water. Neil was similarly
affected and Lyn had torn the bottom section from her housecoat, to protect his thighs from rubbing on the rough sailcloth,
while preserving her own modesty by fabricating a rather
ineffectual bikini from a piece of sail. My shorts had disintegrated, leaving me with underpants only, while Robin and
Sandy preserved their swimsuits intact. The boys had shirts,
and my singlet, though somewhat bloodstained, was still in one
piece.

As the sun crept round to the port side of the raft, and we
lay gasping in the torrid heat, sucking at pieces of rubber trying

to create saliva to ease the burden of our thirst, Lyn quietly arranged the bedding so that we should at least start the night with dry sheets, and then passed the water round for sips. Our eyes followed the movement of the jar to each other's lips, then passing the jar to the twins, Lyn saw that they had a mouthful each, and after wetting her own lips, placed the now empty jar back in its place. I watched the dark shadows under Douglas's eyes as he kept lookout for ships, his mouth working to try to retain the saliva which dispels the foul taste of thirst in a dry mouth. His face had suddenly gone much thinner and the hollowness of his cheeks, clenched against the dryness of his palate, gave his head a skull-like appearance. I shut my eyes and lay back to think out the problem of how to select the fish I wanted to catch without interference from the other varieties. I could only think of one answer, a spear of some description. I had seen plenty of fish spears on my travels, but their strength and design lay in a type of wood that was not available to me. It would need a fairly thick shaft to give strength and the point would have to be reinforced to give the softer wood penetrating power.

As the evening shadows darkened the inside of the raft, I opened another tin of water and decanted it into the jar; Lyn prayed quietly for rain and Robin stared dully at the jar for a moment, then turning his face to the canopy, stuck the tube in his mouth and started blowing. Douglas, sponge in hand, mopped up the sea water in the bottom of the raft while the twins brought out the food boxes ready for the last meal of the day. The breeze blowing gently from the south now died away, leaving the sea almost calm except for the marching swells of the south-east trades, and *Ednamair*'s sail hung limp for the first time since we had started our voyage north. We still had about a hundred and fifty miles of northing to make before we would come under the influence of the Doldrums weather, and with six pints of water left (including the brackish stuff) I wondered if we had come to the end of the road.

We each ate our small piece of fish in silence, and sucked at our small sections of lemon with an ecstasy of taste unequalled in my experience; and we still had one lemon left! Such treasure! We sipped again from the water jar before dark and lay down to ease the long hours of night away, dreaming of ice cream and fresh fruit with a detachment worthy of monastic meditation, for desire had succumbed to rigours of self-denial.

### Seventh day

The windless night filled our ears with unaccustomed silence, and in the quiet of the calm swell the phosphorescent gleam of the large dorado, streaking from under the raft and leaping high into the air, to land in bursting showers of green glowing fire, was a display not often seen by men.

The foul dryness of our mouths aggravated the discomfort of our sleepless bodies as we tried to ease the agony of our thirst, twisting this way and that, then breathlessly we watched the gathering clouds obscure the stars and as dawn paled the eastern horizon, it began to rain, a heavy shower this time, with a steady downpour. Slowly the water in the pipe from the canopy ran clear and we filled our empty cans and spare plastic bags, our bellies and our mouths until we could not force down another drop. We lay with our faces turned to the sky and let the pure fresh water cleanse the salt from our beards and hair; suddenly everything had changed from the shadow of the spectre of death to the joyful prospect of life, and all by a shower of rain. We would make the Doldrums now! We lay uncaring, chewing strips of dorado and revelling in the absence of thirst, talking excitedly of good food and watching the bulging plastic bags swing lazily from the roof of the canopy. We had water!

Douglas, lazily watching the dispersing clouds, suddenly sat up with a start, pointing excitedly. 'A ship! A ship! It's a ship!' We all crowded to the door of the raft, staring in the direction of his pointing finger; a cargo vessel of about six thousand tons was approaching us on a course that would bring her within three miles of us. I felt my heart pound against my ribs. 'Get out the flares,' I said hoarsely, 'and pass them to me in the dinghy, they'll see us better from there.'

Three miles was a fair distance, but on a dull day like this, against a background of rain they should see us easily. I clambered into the dinghy and Douglas passed me the rockets and hand flares; my hands trembled as I ripped open a parachute rocket flare and, with a mute appeal to the thing to fire, struck the igniter on the fuse. It spluttered and hissed, then

roared off on a trajectory high above the raft, its pinkish mag-
nesium flare slowly spiralling downwards leaving a trail of
smoke in the sky. They couldn't fail to see it. I waited a
moment or two watching for the ship to alter course, then
struck a hand flare, holding it high above my head. The
blinding red light was hot to hold and I pointed it away from
the wind to ease my hand, the red embers of the flare dropping
into the dinghy; as it went out I struck another, smoke from
the first now a rising plume in the sky; surely they must see
that. I waited a little, my hands trembling. 'This chance might
not come again,' I said, anxious faces crowding the door of the
raft, 'I'm going to use our last rocket flare and one more hand
flare.' We watched tensely as the second rocket flare soared and
spiralled its gleaming distress message high above us; desperately I struck the third hand flare and held it high, standing on
the thwart and holding on to the mast. 'Look, look, you
bastards!' I shouted. 'Set fire to the sail!' Lyn's voice. I stuck
the flare to the sail but it only melted. The ship sailed on,
slowly disappearing behind a rain shower, and when she
reappeared her hull was half obscured by the horizon, five miles
distant and disappearing fast. The time was eleven o'clock.
My shoulders drooped. 'We daren't use another,' I said. 'They
won't see it now and we have to keep something for the next
one.' We had three hand flares left. Lyn smiled cheerfully. 'It
says in the instruction book that the first one probably wouldn't
see us,' she said slowly, 'and I'd already told the twins not to
expect anything.' She gathered the twins to her, comfortingly.
We stared at the dwindling speck on the horizon and felt so
lonely that it hurt. 'I'm sorry lads,' I felt very tired. 'We used
to consider that one of the most important tenets of good seamanship was "Keep a good lookout". That lot seem to be
pretty poor seamen!'

Our position was 3° North and 240 miles west of Espinosa
(almost 95°20′W) on Wednesday 21 June, midsummer's day,
on the route from Panama to the Marquesas; the ship was
westbound. I surveyed the empty flare cartons bitterly, and the
one smoke flare which was damp and wouldn't work, and something happened to me in that instant, that for me changed the
whole aspect of our predicament. If these poor bloody seamen
couldn't rescue us, then we would have to make it on our own

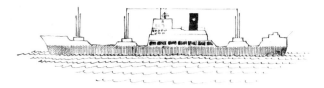

The ship that didn't see us

and to hell with them. We would survive without them, yes,
and that was the word from now on, 'survival', not 'rescue', or
'help', or dependence of any kind, just survival. I felt the
strength flooding through me, lifting me from the depression
of disappointment to a state of almost cheerful abandon. I felt
the bitter aggression of the predator fill my mind. This was not
our environment and the beasts around us would eat us if we
failed. We would carve a place for ourselves amongst them;
they had millions of years of adaptation on their side, but we
had brains and some tools. We would live for three months or
six months from the sea if necessary, but 'We would get these
boys to land' as Lyn had said, and we would do it ourselves if
there was no other way. From that instant on, I became a savage.

We lunched on dry fish, a half biscuit and a tiny piece of
glucose each to cheer us up, followed by a good mouthful of
water, after which I returned to the *Ednamair* to clear up the
debris of empty cases and burnt powder. When I returned to
the raft I said: 'From now on we have a new password; we
forget words like rescue for we can expect none, and think of
existence only in terms of survival.' Lyn nodded immediately.
'What's the password for today?' she called to the twins—
'Survival' they echoed, and they seemed to understand that
it was no longer a question of 'if' we would reach land, but 'when'.
Robin seemed to regard our change of attitude with mild indifference, but in Douglas's eyes I could see that the shadow of
the ship's passing would haunt him for the rest of his days.

The wind rose from the south again after the passage of rain
and I decided to stream the sea anchor, to hold the raft in the
shipping route, for forty-eight hours I was tempted to carry
straight on but rescue is, after all, part of the survival exercise
and I would at least pay lip service to the ordinary practices

of seamen. In two days the current would have carried us
beyond the shipping lane and we could then proceed on our
voyage to the coast. The sea anchor streamed and the sail
reefed, I had just returned to the raft when an excited call
from Sandy, watching the sea anchor's mushroom trailing
behind us, brought us to the after door of the raft. A huge
hammerhead shark glided six feet below, its wicked eye leering
up at us. The twins gazed down at it fascinated, not in the
least afraid, and discussed its more dangerous man-eating practices with Douglas as dispassionately as if they were visiting an
aquarium on an afternoon outing.

Towards late afternoon we felt an unusually hard bump on
the raft floor, unlike the quick thrust of the striking dorado,
and poking our heads out of the stern door of the raft we found
ourselves gazing at the large scaly head of a turtle, protruding
eyes set above a nasty-looking beak, surveying us with a dis-
passionate unblinking scrutiny. The day before I would have
said, 'Leave it, we can't manage that,' but now things were
different. 'We'll have this one,' I said. 'Let's get it aboard the
dinghy.' The turtle's flippers had become entangled in the sea
anchor line, so first passing a rope from the dinghy under the
raft, we made it fast to one of the back flippers, then, carefully
avoiding the searching beak, freed the turtle from the sea
anchor rope and towed it around the raft to the *Ednamair*. I
scrambled on to the dinghy and pulled the now struggling
turtle alongside, reaching down to grasp the back flippers. I
twisted the turtle round until its back was next to the dinghy
and heaved. It was surprisingly heavy and as it came aboard,
the dinghy tilted alarmingly. I threw my weight to the other
side to trim her, then with a bump and a thrashing of claws
the reptile lay on its back in the bottom of the dinghy, all
eighty pounds of it. I put my thumbs up to the twins and
Douglas watching from the raft, and they cheered excitedly.

Now for the difficult bit. I looked at the armoured amphibian
with a farmer's eye; where to cut to reach the artery? I had
helped to slaughter a few pigs and lambs and had a pretty
good idea how to tackle this one. I grasped the pointed knife
in my right hand and, putting a foot on each of the front
flippers, held its beak with my left hand, then plunged the
knife into the leathery skin of the neck, deep into the spinal

column, then with quick, outward strokes of the knife to right
and left I cut both vein and artery. Deep red blood spurted
into the bottom of the dinghy and gradually, beak and flippers
ceased thrashing as the beast died. Apart from a few minor
scratches I was unscathed, so in the gathering dusk I washed
the blood from my hands into the bottom of the dinghy, careful
not to spill any in the water. I didn't want to bring any
inquisitive sharks around, especially our hammerheaded friend,
until we had started moving again, for if they suspected that
the blood came from the raft they would probably attack the
inflatable with disastrous consequences. Excitedly we discussed
this addition to our larder. Lyn had heard from someone that
turtle livers were inedible so we decided to discard the offal
rather than risk illness. Twenty-four hours previously I would
not have had the stomach for such a bloody business but the
laws of survival applied and the first principle, 'The fittest survive, the weakest go to the wall', had now become our way of
life. We would struggle and endure and if our reflexes were
not as swift as the animals and fish around us, we had cunning,
and we would improve with practice.

The wind steadily increased during the evening and the sea
became noisy about the raft again. Inside, bodies twisted and

10-foot Hammerheaded Shark, another man-eating companion

turned restlessly seeking a comfortable position, for only the
twins were small enough to lie down full length on the floor.
Water slopped around the depressions made by hip-bones and
elbows in the inflated rubber flooring and the sound of the
watchkeeper blowing up the flotation chambers became just
another sound in the night to those who tried to rest. To the
watchkeeper, it was an exhausting routine of bailing and blowing which left the mouth sore, the hands cramped and the tiny
pimples, forerunners of salt water boils, stinging on hands, feet,
legs, arms and buttocks. We sometimes found time to look
around for ships!

### Eighth day

As dawn broke and we awoke again to the realisation that the
ship had not seen us, Lyn called from her watchkeeping at the
doorway: 'What's the password for the day?' The answer
'Survival' came with surprising vigour from us all and we set
about the morning chores of mopping up and drying bedding
with a cheerfulness scarcely appropriate to our desperate situation. I went over to *Ednamair* to dress the turtle. It took me
an hour and a half to remove the belly shell, sawing and
hacking with the knife blade which grew blunter as the shell
seemed to grow thicker; finally with a bit of undercutting, I
managed to lift the shell off and set about extracting the meat.
The turtle has a poor killing out ratio, about twenty-five per
cent to thirty per cent, and has its joints in the most inaccessible
places. It took me another hour to hack out the shoulder meat
and that surrounding the back flipper bones. I opened the
stomach and found, to my delight, a golden cascade of a
hundred or so yellow egg yolks awaiting collection. I cut some
meat from the shoulder piece and then with a couple of dozen
eggs in a dish returned to the raft for breakfast where all waited
curiously for their first taste of turtle meat.

As we all eyed the raw meat with some distaste, a Grace of
Robert Burns came to my mind and I quoted:

> 'Some hae meat and canna eat,
> Some hae nane and want it,
> But we hae meat and we can eat,
> So let the Lord be thanked.'

Neil grinned and sank his teeth into a piece of steak. 'Good' was all he said, and we all fell to with a will. We swallowed the egg yolks, bursting them like yellow plums inside our mouths and allowing their creamy richness to permeate our taste buds, enjoying the flavour of the raw food as only starving people can. Robin declined the eggs—too rich for him—but chewed vigorously at the tender meat declaring that he enjoyed his steaks done 'rare'. Douglas, Lyn and Sandy, after some initial distaste, chewed at the pieces of meat with increasing interest as rejection of the idea of raw meat gave way to acceptance of the taste of it. We washed it down with a draught of water and lay back and reflected on our good fortune. If we could catch turtles, and rain, we would survive alright; I thought of the fish spear; with turtles and dorado, we'd be wealthy!

After discussing the day's work with Douglas and Robin, I returned to the dinghy and carefully skinned the flippers, head (Douglas wanted it for a souvenir) and neck, and loosened the offal from the shell ready to tip over the side when we started moving again. Next, the meat was cut from the bones and then divided into small pieces which were laid out across the thwart to dry in the sun. We had about twenty pounds of meat and bone altogether, and *Ednamair* looked like a slaughter-house, but there were also the dorado strips, now nearly dry again after their wetting and tasting very pleasantly too! The huge turtle shell lay in the bottom of the dinghy, like a small bath, and I tried to imagine uses to which it could be put. My primary thought was that I would be able to use a piece to arm the spear but the knife was too blunt to be of use in shaping the barbs and the shell itself would be too brittle when dried out, and not hard enough if it was kept wet. With the meat nicely drying my return to the raft with another meal was hailed with interest and lunch time found us happily gnawing bones. With the inside of the raft shaped like a cave, it was not difficult to imagine that we had dropped a few thousand years in time, for not only did we look like cave dwellers, I, at least, felt like one.

The temperature of the sea had risen by several degrees, a sign I had been watching for to indicate that we were no longer under the influence of the Humboldt current, but our noon position, after a night at sea anchor in relatively quiet weather, had changed little from the previous day. I therefore recorded it in my 'log' as 3° North, 240 miles west of Espinosa, the same as the day before. (My log book had, of course, been lost with *Lucette*, but I was keeping a scrap log round the edges of the pages of the instruction book.)

At intervals during the afternoon I crossed to the *Ednamair* to turn over the drying turtle meat, hanging some on the stays and the mast. Since we now had an interest in dry weather as well as the other variety, we comforted ourselves, in the heat of the day, with the thought that the turtle meat and fish would benefit, if we didn't. Watchkeepers also had a dual reason for looking out for rain showers, for the meat had to be brought under cover before it rained.

Douglas and Robin had been investigating the influx of water into the raft again and a small hole which had developed in the thin fabric was plugged with a bobbin of cotton thread and the flow had been reduced, if not entirely eliminated. The flotation chambers lost a great deal of pressure through the fabric on a hot day and this had to be constantly replaced by blowing, keeping the raft as rigid as possible to avoid wear by flexing and rubbing. So while I worked at providing food, Lyn and the boys worked hard at keeping the raft afloat and as dry as possible. Lyn's day was full to overflowing, not only with keeping the twins occupied but also with tending to our various ailments, which were becoming more numerous with the onset of skin eruptions due to salt water immersion. She insisted on a daily routine of leg and arm exercises for the twins regardless of their protests, and saw that the bedding was dried each morning in spite of the fact that it was soaked again shortly after it was placed over us; that first feeling of snuggling down under dry sheets meant a lot to us.

Only Robin had executed a bowel movement since the *Lucette* was sunk, and that shortly after joining the raft, so Lyn was already agitating for a tube to be found, suitable for her to administer enemas, so that the unpalatable, brackish water could be administered rectally in the form of water retention enemas, and while I was rather perturbed at the engineering problems involved, I felt the idea was a good one.

More serious was Lyn's anxiety over Neil's listlessness and his quicker deterioration in body condition than the rest of us,

probably due to his initial seasickness, and we discussed extra
rations for the twins; finally we agreed that as long as we could
obtain food from the sea, the emergency rations should be kept
as supplementary rations for the twins only, for their digestions
were less likely to cope with the raw food in the way that our
adult bodies could do.

As we lay down to rest that evening, we had resolved many
of our doubts and anxieties, but more unsettling problems were
already looming larger on the horizon; how much longer
would the raft last? How often would we catch a turtle? How
long could we do without vitamin C without deterioration to
scurvy? There were a thousand and one questions and no text
books in which to look for the answers.

### Ninth day

The south-east trade winds increased to a freshening force five
breeze during the night, keeping the watchkeepers busy with
the bailer as the raft jerked uneasily between the sea anchor
on one side and the pull of *Ednamair* on the other; the temperature of the sea water had grown noticeably cooler again indicating that we were still within the influence of the westerly set
of the Humboldt current. Although we had no means of steering
the raft, it was possible for me to angle the sail so that the
dinghy pulled it across the wind at an angle of about forty-
five degrees. We relied, initially, on observation of sun and
stars for direction, and once having found the relevant direction
of the underlying swell, used it to record our course without
reference to the sun which climbed overhead at noon, or the
wind, which could change unnoticed. The wind was fairly
consistent in its south-easterly origin, but it would not always
be so, especially on reaching the Doldrums, and I wanted
Douglas to be able to determine his direction without its help
or mine in case, for any reason, I wasn't there to give it.

I estimated our noon position at 3°10′ North, 243 miles west
of Espinosa and with morning chores over we lunched on a
little dried dorado, some half-dry turtle which tasted much
nicer than the raw stuff but, of course, required more water
to digest it, and a small piece of onion of which we had two
left; it made a pleasant change from our tiny piece of biscuit.
We also concocted an egg-nog from a dozen turtle eggs, a cup

of water, a little glucose and a sprinkling of dried yeast; Robin
had admitted an aversion to turtle eggs but he drank his share of
this mixture with relish; indeed, we all enjoyed the new flavour.

The afternoon was hot. The sun's rays radiated through the
double canopy with savage intensity as we lay around in listless
repose waiting for evening to bring earth's grateful shadow from
the sun. I was lying near the canopy door, my forearm seeking
the salt water coolness of the leaking floor when my hand came
in contact with the cotton plug. A swift pull brought water
flooding into the raft and Robin started up in alarm. 'Come
on, we're going to have a bath. You first!' I filled the bailer
with cool sea water and poured it over him—'My God, that's
wonderful.' He revelled in the three inches of seawater in the
forward section of the inflatable. I sloshed water on all of them
as they took turns to splash in the flooded section, pouring it
over their heads in a cooling stream. The sharks might make
it too dangerous to swim outside the raft but there was no
reason why we shouldn't enjoy a shower. After Robin had
soaked me in turn, the plug was put back and the water bailed
out again. We all felt much better, and Lyn and the twins,
busy with a pencil and some sailcloth, had set about designing
a greenhouse in which they were going to grow tomatoes when
they returned to Leek in Staffordshire. Douglas preoccupied
his mind with visions of roasted rabbit, which he had never
seen or tasted but was quite certain it would be his ideal dish.
We began to think seriously about food, not just eating it but
growing and preparing it down to the tiniest detail, and this
led Robin and Douglas into a marathon memory game about
Mrs Brown's shopping list which reached a massive total of
thirty-two articles before Robin won (largely by his purchase
of some unpronounceable books on statistics). I felt that their
minds weren't suffering a great deal even if their bones had
become a little more obvious.

The seas had roughened considerably during the afternoon
and by evening the raft corkscrewed heavily on the steep waves;
*Ednamair* yawed widely under her reefed down sail and I decided
to take it down altogether for the night to ease the strain on the
sea anchor rope at the other end of the raft. I checked the
fastenings and felt thankful that we had the strong towing wire
to hold us together. We were now making way in spite of the

sea anchor, and the strain on the after towing straps, to which
the sea anchor was attached, was considerable with the raft
making a lot of water as the seas broke on to it. The floor had
to be bailed every ten minutes to keep us from lying in water
and the flotation chambers lost pressure so quickly that blowing
them up became an extension of breathing. A quick check on
the rubber stopper showed that the nylon binding had cut
through the already worn fabric around the hole in the flotation
chamber so it was bound with tape, which reduced the air loss,
until daylight. The dinghy was still full of turtle blood and
offal which I dared not dump until we were moving at a
reasonable speed for fear of shark attack, and it yawed sluggishly in the steep seas, shipping some water as it lay broadside.
I decided that it was safer to risk the sea anchor than the
dinghy so I hoisted the reefed down sail again, which involved
some strenuous acrobatics boarding the dinghy and returning
to the raft.

I talked quietly with Douglas during the evening. He was
still depressed by the failure of the ship to pick us up and
probably realised, more than Robin could do, what this meant
in terms of future rescue; the advent of auto-pilots, gyro-
compass and other modern electronic aids to navigation on
ships had eliminated the presence of the human eye; the rubber
raft and the fibreglass dinghy were poor reflectors of radar
echoes and would not be picked up on radar screens except
at very close range and only then if they could be excluded
from the sea clutter. Indeed, if the standard of watchkeeping
was as poor on other ships as on the one that had passed us
yesterday, we stood a better chance of being run down than
picked up!

Clouds thickened in the northern sky as another extensive
occluded front passed over; the wind became a gentle breeze
again and the seas subsided; though clouds obscured the stars
for most of the night, no rain fell and we were afforded a more
comfortable night than we had expected from its beginning.

### *Tenth day*

As soon as daylight had faded the stars from the clearing skies,
we tripped and housed the sea anchor, shook the reef out of

the sail and continued on our way to the Doldrums. We had
paid lip service to the standard practices of rescue by remaining
in the shipping lane for as long as we could, but I felt that our
present circumstances called for more than standard practice
and was anxious that no more time should be wasted, for we
were still some distance from the rain area and our stocks of
water were dwindling once more.

As soon as we were moving again I dumped the offal and
bailed the blood out of the dinghy; dozens of scavenger fish
appeared from nowhere, the sea swirling as they fought to
devour the scraps of coagulated turtle blood. In a few minutes,
the now familiar fins of four sharks were seen as they cruised
around looking for the source of the blood. The sea boiled as
one of them attacked a dorado, the shark leaping its full ten-
foot length clear of the water in a tremendous strike. Although
they were our constant reminders of what lay in store for us
if we failed, we could not help admiring the beautiful streamlined shape of these white-tipped sharks as they cruised in
smooth unhurried serenity with their attendant bevies of pilot
fish close to the raft. Our admiration did not deter me from
thumping one of them with a paddle when it came too close
(it beat a hasty retreat) and as if they had taken the hint we
weren't troubled by any of the others, but from then onwards
we were never without at least one shark in attendance.

At 3°30′ North and 250 miles west of Cape Espinosa, our
noon position confirmed that the Doldrums, a mere ninety
miles now, were well within striking distance and that our first
leg of the journey was nearly over. High cirrus clouds moved
contrary to the trade winds, their unsubstantial vapours con-
veying little to the searcher for weather signs, and I turned my
attention to the dinghy, scraping out the turtle shell and
collecting all the pieces of bone from the flippers. The half-
cured meat had turned a deep brown colour under the heat
of the sun and I took a little of it back to the raft, to spin out
our luncheon of flipper bones and eggs.

During the afternoon the plug in the bottom of the raft was
dislodged and water flooded into the forward compartment
through a now much enlarged hole. We plugged it eventually
by ramming an aircraft dinghy instruction book, made of
waterproof material, into the hole, a creditable use for it, and

while Robin bailed the compartment dry again, I wondered how long it would be before the raft became untenable altogether and we became dependent on *Ednamair* for our lives. There was no doubt in my mind that we should have to do this eventually, but the prospect of the six of us fitting into, and living in, the confined limits of the nine foot six inch boat along with our food and water supplies and other items of equipment apalled me, for the slightest imbalance would bring the sea flooding in over the small freeboard.

The lifebelts, which were filled with kapok, had been used as pillows, and for keeping our bodies from lying in the pools of water which collected in the raft during the night, but now they had become so saturated that I took them over to the dinghy and placed them between the thwarts to dry out. In the meanwhile, we again searched for leaks, for there was one, as yet unlocated, in the after section which was causing us much bodily discomfort. I decided we would have to rip the side screens out of the raft to find the leak which was coming from under them and set about doing this before darkness fell, using the blunt-nosed raft knife for the purpose to avoid cutting into any of the flotation chambers.

The continuous contact with the salt water had aggravated our skin eruptions and we all suffered from an increasing number of salt water boils on our arms and legs, shoulders and buttocks; they were extremely painful when brought in contact with the terylene sail and other rough objects, and would soon present an additional health hazard unless we could keep out of the sea water and stop the eruptions spreading.

We were still examining the raft inch by inch when daylight faded and we settled down to another comfortless night, the constant plying of the bailing cup broken only when the watchkeeper stopped to blow up the flotation chambers.

### *Eleventh day*

My morning inspection of the dinghy after a weary night of tossing and turning, drying out and getting wet again, started with the discovery that the petrol can had vanished during the night. We hadn't seen it go and although I felt that we could have used the container for water, the loss wasn't really a tragic one and was shortly afterwards alleviated by the discovery of two flying fish. We valued these tasty morsels as much as the dorado did, and as long as there were flying fish around, the bigger fish would also be with us. True, we hadn't found a way of catching them yet, but another one might jump into the dinghy, and I was about to start work on a spear.

After breakfast, for which we used our last lemon and the remaining scraps of bad onion, I went over to *Ednamair* and dumped the scrapings from the turtle shell and cleaned the inside of the boat thoroughly from the turtle blood which still adhered in places. Douglas gave it a final scrub and then we stored the dried meat and fish in one of the boxes, placing the turtle shell over it for a lid. We were ready for rain if it came, in more ways than one, for we were down to twelve pints of fresh water again and would have to reduce our ration unless another active front passed over.

Our position at 4° North and 250 miles west of Espinosa seemed to coincide with the sort of weather we were experiencing, occluded fronts moving southwards from the Doldrums passed over with greater frequency now and although rain was still denied us, we were grateful for these signs that rain did lie ahead, not too far distant, and we were moving towards it. The sea water temperature had risen at least ten degrees in the last twenty-four hours indicating that we were now out of the Humboldt at last, and while I could not be sure we were in the counter current until we reached a latitude above 5°30′ North, at least I could discount any further westerly drift in my dead reckoning calculations. A moderate breeze was still blowing us northwards at a rate of twenty-four miles a day and with an allowance for local set and drift, I hoped we would be within the environs of the Doldrums in two days. The spectre of a waterless week haunted us more than any other hazard, for water shortage left us weak and incompetent, breathless on the slightest exertion, and we knew vaguely that the process of dehydration, once started, was difficult to correct and not just a matter of drinking extra water when it became available.

We had given up looking for the leak into the after section of the raft, and during the morning played Twenty Questions and talked about food. Robin described his travels in Ireland and I described my youthful days with the Boy Scouts, camping

and exploring in the Highlands of Scotland. The twins readily
absorbed themselves in our adventures and created a bridge
of contemporary companionship with us across the years. Now
that *Lucette* was gone, they wanted to get back to their old life
in Britain, and they listened avidly to the adventures of city
youngsters in the country as if they too had never known
country life. For them there would never be another *Lucette*,
but they were quite confident that, when they grew up, they
would sail their own boat around the world like the Australian
twins we had met, on their ketch *Metung*, when we had visited
Jamaica. The *Lucette* would live on in the twins' memory and
they would always remember her gentle lines and robust build.
They were perturbed that we had not gone round the world
as we had said we would do, but I felt that the important
objectives had already been achieved in the widening of the
horizons of their minds, for they were no longer afraid of
meeting people whose language and customs were different,
nor did they think that because they were different they were
inferior.

Robin puffed steadily at the flotation compartment—he was
twice as good now as when he first tried, although there was
still plenty of room for improvement; then Douglas's bellows
took over and the valve squealed as he pushed massive breaths
into the tube. The flotation chambers grew firm and rounded,
the canopy's arched support became rigid under the increased
pressure; it was late afternoon and we were ready for rain if
the mushrooming cumulus decided to precipitate in our
direction. Taking the spare paddle handle, I crossed to the
*Ednamair*, cut a piece of wood from one of the boxes and
settled down to carve the head of a fish spear which would
later be fitted into the paddle handle shaft. I was still whittling
as dusk closed in and already the grain of the wood showed
smooth and streamlined round the angles of the first barb. Two
notches angled towards each other were carved into the point
ready to receive the armour of nails.

Sleeping space was now very cramped as we lay on top of
the flotation chambers to try to keep clear of the water in the
bottom of the raft, so I decided to ease the situation by sleeping
in the dinghy; Sandy came with me and after we had settled
down on the hard fibreglass hull we realised that the inflatable

was much kinder to our bones and as we clutched the sailcloth sheets to us, warmer as well. We spent an uneasy night trying to find comfort for our tender, boil-infested bodies, finally snatching a few moments of exhausted slumber just before dawn. For those on the raft the routine of blowing and bailing went on, spurred by the tyranny of survival's only alternative.

### Twelfth day

Daybreak came slowly under a gloomy sky, typical Doldrums weather, and as we stirred to the harsh commands of self-preservation our eyes sought the horizon, the sea, the dinghy, searching for rain, danger and food. I returned to the raft with Sandy to find Robin blowing hard to inflate the after section of the raft which sagged in a dismal droop, the archway support of the canopy nearly touching the floor. We blew alternately until the support was rigid again and though I searched the outside no other leak than the inaccessible one was evident; it was probably getting worse, but since we couldn't reach it we would just have to blow a little more often.

The morning routine of clearing the water and the saturated bedding from the raft was occupying more of our time as conditions worsened, and we were becoming slower in performing even small tasks. Lyn had to scold us all to get us to co-operate in clearing the raft and tending to our sores. She cleaned the pus from our eyes and we groaned and snapped as she nagged us into ordinary routines of body hygiene and exercise. We all cheered when it started to rain, but fell silent again as the thinning stratus cloud precipitated in such scanty quantities that it scarcely wet the canopy and none ran through the tube from the catchment area above us. Lyn once more prayed that we might have enough rain to sustain life, and as the clouds thinned and moved away Robin made a trite and uncalled for remark about the power of Lyn's prayer. I felt anger surge through me at this display of intolerance, and had difficulty in restraining myself from taking savage revenge on his impertinence, contenting myself with pointing out that as the democratic freedom to worship was just as important as the freedom not to worship, we could be spared his unsavoury remarks. Robin looked owlishly at me as the import of my tone rather than my words reached him and he apologised to Lyn for his rudeness.

My spear was finished by the early afternoon and after varnishing the bindings of the nails on the tip to smooth the point, I surveyed my handiwork with some misgivings. It looked alright and that was just about all I could say for it. As soon as the varnish was dry, I made one or two experimental thrusts at the turtle shell, then turning to see if there were any dorado around, knocked the point against the mast and broke it off at the barb. My language blistered the air and Douglas was sufficiently moved to remark that it was better than losing it in a fish. I immediately started on my second model, this time hacking a piece of wood from the cypress wood thwart, a tough stringy wood, for my purpose. The absence of sun allowed me to work throughout the afternoon and while the dinghy was fairly steady in the gentle breeze and smooth sea, I could work more comfortably. At tea time, I made ready to return to the raft and pulling on the towrope found to my surprise that it pulled away from the raft and plopped into the sea. The shackle pin had worked loose and had fallen out, and as I paddled back to the raft I reflected on our good fortune that this hadn't happened during the night in stormy weather, for to lose the dinghy now was to lose our lives; not only was our dried food stored in it, but also the refilled water cans which had plugs in, for they stood upright in the dinghy whereas they were continually being knocked over in the raft, with consequent leakage. I secured the end of the towrope to the towing strap and lashed the half hitches with twine, then took the small lifeline and secured it between dinghy and raft as a precaution in case anything similar happened again, for there were too many sharks around to go swimming.

The bottom of the raft was now continually wet and our boils developed and spread at a disquieting speed, causing acute discomfort wherever we came in contact with anything; to have a piece of terylene sail drawn across one's skin resulted in minutes of agony so we now moved slowly and with caution to avoid unnecessary suffering, but in the darkness changing watch became an agonised exercise for everyone; it was obvious to us all that unless we could keep drier, we would be unwilling, if not unable to do anything for fear of hurting ourselves. Bailing was now carried out almost continuously, the bailer being passed from one end of the raft to the other as each compartment required attention, and blowing up the flotation chambers was now almost second nature to us. Our talk no longer centred round the possibility of rescue but rather on how long it was going to take us to reach land and what sort of condition we would be in when we reached it.

Lyn talked with the twins endlessly of their grandfather's cottage on the quiet reaches of a small canal in Staffordshire, and of how he would have enjoyed hearing of our adventures across the different countries we had visited. 'Old Pev', as Lyn's father was affectionately known to us all, had died with quiet courage, a few months before we started our world voyage, and had followed his own recipe for life, 'You've got to get up to survive', until his cancerous body could no longer house his great spirit.

The sky had cleared at sunset and there was now no trace of raincloud as twilight deepened the velvet darkness of the Pacific night. Sandy and I had decided to stay on the raft for this night; the memory of our discomfort the night before was still fresh in our minds and the kindly touch of the inflated fabric on the raft was distinctly preferable to the unyielding

5-foot Mako Shark—quite an armful

fibreglass of the dinghy, even if it was dry. I was on watch
between nine and eleven that night and as I finished my bailing
for a few minutes, a fish splashed noisily beside the raft. I
looked down and dropped my arm into the water, hand taut
like a claw, and hoped that coincidence would bring my hand
in contact with the right part of the dorado to let me pull it
aboard. I had touched their backs a time or two but always
in the wrong place, but I'm an optimist when it comes to
catching food and I felt sure that sooner or later it had to
happen. I picked up the bailer and was about to start bailing
again when there was a loud splash and again the raft trembled
under a blow from a large fish. I was tensed ready when the
fish jumped a third time; it landed against the side of the raft
just under my right arm. I hooked my right arm under it and
grabbed quickly with my left hand, then feeling the unslippery
skin looked down at the white belly and U-shaped mouth of a
five foot shark lying docile in my arms like a baby. Realising
that one slash of that mouth would finish the raft completely,
I dropped it as if it was a red hot poker; it snapped its savage
jaws, struck the raft a blow with its tail and was gone. Thankfully I resumed bailing. We didn't want to evacuate just yet!

### Thirteenth day

The morning started well with the discovery of two flying fish
in the dinghy which, together with the one which had landed
in the raft, made us breakfast of half a fish each. Though they
were very small, they were sweet tasting and contained fresh
water so we saved a sip from the water jar. We were still on a
voluntary system of rationing but I watched each person drink,
more to reassure myself that they were taking their share rather
than the reverse. On two occasions Lyn put the jar to her lips
and did not drink, and when told to drink, she protested that
she didn't need it and the twins could have her share. I knew
the children needed her as much as the water and put down
my best argument, none for anybody until she drank.

I took the three flying fish heads over to *Ednamair* to use as
bait for fishing while I finished my second spear, and the boys
occupied themselves bailing, blowing and looking for leaks. Lyn

did the morning chores—washing clothes and drying bedding, giving the twins their leg exercises.

The first head was quickly taken by scavenger fish so I baited the hook with the second head and placed it deep, hoping the sharks would be elsewhere. To my surprise, I had a strike and a few moments later a two-pound fish lay flapping in the bottom of the boat, shouts of encouragement coming from the raft. I fixed the third flying fish head on and sent it deep again and looked at my catch as I waited for another strike; the fish I had caught still flapped wildly in the bottom of the dinghy, so taking up the knife to put it out of its misery, I severed the head with a quick twist of the knife. I gaped at the short stump of knife left in my hand and at the remaining six inches of blade lying in the bottom of the boat, unable to understand that I had broken it by cutting a small fish's head off, and was still gazing at it in resentment when the second strike jerked my attention to the line. A big one this time, it fought strongly and the line cut into my hands as foot by foot I pulled the fish in towards the dinghy. Robin and the twins watched excitedly from the raft door; I could see the fish now, a twenty pounder of the mackerel type, fighting and struggling as I dragged it to the surface, then as I pulled sharply to bring the fish into the boat, it gave a mighty lunge into the air and was gone, the empty hook no longer curved but almost straightened by the dynamic force of the fish's leap. My disappointment was so intense and the pain from the crushed boils on my fingers so severe that I would have wept if I had had any moisture to spare for tears. As it was, I put a larger hook on the line and baiting it with some offal from the dead two pounder, sent it deep again determined to play it first this time and risk it being taken by sharks. The strike came almost immediately and slowly I pulled my severed line in; the sharks were back already!

I had two large hooks left and as I watched the long sleek shape of the sharks glide slowly by I resolved to keep them for another day. One shark turned again and cruised at a leisurely speed towards the dinghy, its fin knifing the surface of the sea. I grabbed the spear and struck savagely at its snout as it went past; the surprised shark flipped its tail wildly and dived deep, the two others cruising not far behind keeping a respectful distance as I made the transit back to the raft with the newly caught fish for our lunch.

Tempers were frayed when I returned, Robin being particularly uncooperative as Lyn tried to get him to help with the drying of the bedding, and she insisted on the thing being done right if it was done at all. I spoke sharply to Robin reminding him that whilst we realised that things must be very difficult for him as a newcomer to the sea, he must help as best he could. I tried not to ask him to do things which were outside the scope of his practical ability but the things which Lyn asked of him took no skill and gave much comfort.

I turned away from him to look at the twins; Neil, painfully thin, and Sandy were putting the odds and ends back into the raft pocket after Lyn had cleared it of pieces of sodden wrapping paper and empty flare cases. Lyn and I often indulged in some fierce backbiting which our children usually endured with stoical indifference (though Douglas now joined in at times) but they all knew the difference between inconsequential nagging and instructions which had to be carried out for their own good. Robin didn't. At twenty-two, through little fault of his own, he was the product of an eight-year educational system which gave its students little opportunity to learn the basic tenets of physical existence and thrust them into life, unpractical, self-opinionated, and with a fund of prepacked knowledge that is about as useless as a heifer in a hayfield when lives are at stake. I felt sorry that we should be the catalyst which would open his mind to reality but hoped that his sense of justice (Robin always tried to mediate when Lyn and I were at odds with each other) and his sober good nature would help his understanding. I looked at him—'We all have to do things we don't like, Robin, especially now. Left to your own devices you would be dead already.' He opened his mouth to argue but I held up my hand. 'If any one of us dies because you don't feel like doing what you're told, I'll kill you!' His startled eyes came into focus as he stared at me. 'I mean that as a promise, Robin, not a threat,' and he could see that I did.

Our position at noon was 4°45' North, 250 miles west of Espinosa, and though the sea temperature was very warm, I still made no allowance for the easterly set, remembering that it was better for us to sight land before we expected rather

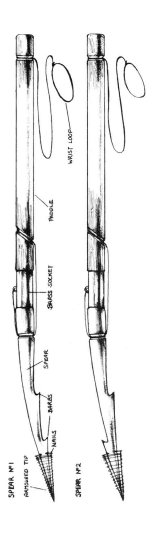

Improvised spears

than after; I had to be sure we were in the current before allowing for it.

After another unsuccessful attempt to stop the water leaks we blew up the flotation chambers working as a team, blowing hard for thirty breaths then passing the tube to the next man. Cumulus was building into heavy cloud again and the probability of rain showers was good. Douglas was exhausted, he put his whole energy into his work and the deep shadows under his eyes betrayed the drain on his physical resources which this imposed. I felt I could see the shadow of death behind the sunken cheeks. Lyn worked steadily at the other end of the raft preparing the twins' little bit of extra food and carefully rewrapping the boxes in their waterproof bags.

Anxiously we watched as the rain showers developed around us, we counted as many as ten at one time, but they all missed and we opened another tin of water for supper; it was only half full! Six pints left and two of these brackish and foul.

I had become used to doing without sleep but there was little sleep for any of us that night, and the youngsters could ill afford the loss. We listened to Lyn talking to the twins about the cottage on the canal, about chickens, rabbits, gardens, anything to keep their minds from contemplating the absence of that most precious of minerals, water. We passed the foul yellow stuff around for sips during the night and imagined ourselves in beautiful cool gardens full of fruits and fountains.

My spear was ready to use, I would try it on the dorado in the morning (I would have tried it that night but the angle of strike was deceptive in the dark). We needed the water these fish contained, if there was to be no rain; I resolved that the water ration would have to be reduced as well and toyed with the idea of distributing it in equal amounts to ensure that we all had our share, but felt that this was a step to be avoided if possible.

### Fourteenth day

The beautiful starlit night shone sparkles of stars on the quiet swells of the now distant trade winds, and seemed to mock our feeble struggle for existence in the raft; to become one with the night would be so easy. We blew, and bailed the forward section

continually, and when Sandy found the hole which leaked into
the after section, surrounded by transparently thin fabric, I felt
that this was the beginning of the end of the raft. I knew that
it was unlikely that I would be able to plug this one, and yet
if I left it, it would certainly split open in the next heavy sea.
I made a plug and inserted it into the hole, tape ready to bind
it if it held. The hole split across and water flooded into the
after compartment; I rammed the plug home in disgust and
stopped enough of the water to bail the compartment dry but
the raft would now need constant bailing at both ends. Apart
from discomfort, my only real opposition to abandoning the
raft was because it would mean abandoning the shelter afforded
by the canopy, so I decided to think of a way of fastening the
canopy on the dinghy to give us continuing shelter from the
sun if we had to abandon.

We had a sip of water for breakfast with no dried food to
detract from its value, after which I crossed to the dinghy to
try for a dorado. The heat of the sun's rays beat on my head
like a club and my mouth, dry like lizard skin, felt full of my
tongue; the slightest exertion left me breathless. I picked up
the spear; the dorado were all deep down as if they knew I
was looking for them. A bump at the stern of the raft attracted
Sandy's attention. 'Turtle!' he yelled. This one was much
smaller than the first and with great care it was caught and
passed through the raft—with Douglas guarding its beak, and
the others its claws, from damaging the fabric—to me on the
dinghy where I lifted it aboard without much trouble. I wrapped
a piece of tape around the broken knife blade and made the
incision into its throat. 'Catch the blood,' Lyn called from the
raft. 'It should be alright to drink a little.' I held the plastic
cup under the copious flow of blood, the cup filled quickly and
I stuck another under as soon as it was full, then raising the
full cup to my lips, tested it cautiously. It wasn't salty at all!
I tilted the cup and drained it. 'Good stuff!' I shouted. I felt
as if I had just consumed the elixir of life. 'Here, take this,'
and I passed the bailer full of blood, about a pint, into the raft
for the others to drink. Lyn said afterwards she had imagined
that she would have to force it down us and the sight of me,
draining the cup, my moustache dripping blood, was quite
revolting. I don't know what I looked like, but it certainly

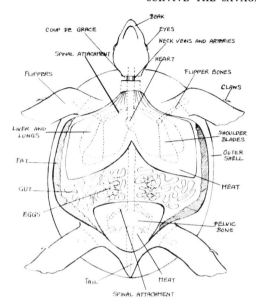

Anatomy of a female turtle (in the stag the tail protrudes beyond the shell)

tasted good, and as the others followed my example it seemed they thought so too. I passed another pint across and though some of this coagulated before it could be drunk, the jelly was cut up and the released serum collected and used as a gravy with the dried turtle and fish.

I set to cutting my way into the turtle much refreshed, and even with the broken knife, made faster work of it than the first one, both because it was smaller, and being younger the shell was not so tough; the fact that I now knew my way around inside a turtle helped a lot too.

The sky was serenely blue that afternoon and with our position worked out at 5°00′ North, 250 miles west of Espinosa, we had arrived at the official limits of the Doldrums. Was this, then, Doldrum weather? Was the 'Rhyme of the Ancient Mariner' right with its 'Nor any drop to drink'? We had four

tins of water left, one of them half sea water, and if any of the
other three contained short measure, well, there might come
another turtle. I looked around the raft at the remains of Robin
and the Robertson family, water wrinkled skin covered with
salt water boils and raw red patches of rash, lying in the bottom
of the raft unmoving except to bail occasionally, and then only
half-heartedly, for the water was cooling in the heat of the day;
our bones showed clearly through our scanty flesh; we had
become much thinner these last few days and our condition
was deteriorating fast. This raft was killing us with its demands
on our energy. Douglas looked across at me, 'Do you think it'll
rain tonight, Dad?' I looked at him and shrugged, looked at
the sky, not a cloud. 'I suppose it could do,' I said. 'Do you
think it will?' he insisted. 'For heaven's sake, Douglas, I'm not
a prophet,' I said testily, 'we'll just have to wait it out.' His
eyes looked hopeless at the blue of the sea from the deep
cavities under his brow; how could I comfort him when he
knew as well as I that it might not rain for a week and that
we'd be dead by then. I said, 'Fresh turtle for tea, we can suck
something out of that.' We could live on turtles, maybe.

We took no water that evening, only a little for the twins.
We talked of the dishes we'd like to eat in the gathering twilight
and I chose fresh fruit salad and ice cream; Lyn, a tin of
apricots; Robin, strawberries and ice cream with milk; Douglas,
the same as me; Neil, chocolate chip ice cream; Sandy, fresh
fruit, ice cream and milk—gallons of ice-cool milk. Later that
night as I took the watch over from Douglas, he described in
detail the dish he had dreamed up during his watch. 'You take
a honeydew melon,' he said. 'Cut the top off and take out the
seeds; that's the dish. Chill it and drop a knob of ice cream in,
then pile in strawberries, raspberries, pieces of apple, pear,
orange, peach and grapefruit, the sweet sort, then cherries and
grapes until the melon is full; pour a lemon syrup over it and
decorate it with chips of chocolate and nuts. Then,' he said
with a dreamy expression on his face, 'You eat it!' 'I'll have
one too,' I said, taking the bailer from his boil-covered hand;
I looked at the sky; to the north-east a faint film of cirrus
stratus cloud dimmed the stars, 'You know, I think it might
rain by morning.' I could feel him relax in the darkness; his
voice came slowly, 'I'll be alright if it doesn't, Dad,' he said.

I started to bail mechanically. We would have to abandon the raft, soon, I thought, and that meant ditching all the unnecessary stuff overboard; in the dinghy there was only room for food, water, flares and us. We'd start to sort things out in the morning.

### Fifteenth day

I watched the cloud develop slowly and drift across the night sky, blotting out the stars one by one. Was it another occluded front? I watched the fish surge out from under the raft, touched one as I tried to grab it, then, the memory of the shark strong in my mind, drew back. I bailed and blew until Lyn took over; I pointed to the thickening cloud: 'Maybe we'll get something to drink out of that.'

It rained at dawn, beautiful, gorgeous rain. We saved three and a half gallons and drank our fill besides; the wind, from the south, freshened a little and as the weather cleared we lay back and enjoyed the sensation of being without thirst, bailing and blowing unheeded for the moment. We talked of the ship that didn't see us, for that had happened after the last rain, and argued whether it would have seen us better if it had been night time. The twins were talking when Douglas, on watch, his voice desperate with dismay, called: 'Dad, the dinghy's gone!' I was across the raft in an instant. I looked at the broken end of wire trailing in the water, the broken line beside it. The dinghy was sixty yards away, sailing still and our lives were sailing away with it; I was the fastest swimmer, no time for goodbyes, to hell with sharks; the thoughts ran through my head as I was diving through the door, my arms flailing into a racing crawl even as I hit the water. I heard Lyn cry out but there was no time for talk. Could I swim faster than the dinghy could sail, that was the point; I glanced at it as I lifted my head to breathe, the sail had collapsed as the dinghy yawed, I moved my arms faster, kicked harder, would the sharks let me, that was another point; my belly crawled as I thought of the sharks, my arms moved faster still; I glanced again, only thirty yards to go but she was sailing again, I felt no fatigue, no cramped muscles, my body felt like a machine as I thrashed my way through the sea only one thought now in mind, the dinghy or us. Then I was there; with a quick heave I flipped over the stern of the dinghy to safety, reached up and tore down the sail before my knees buckled and I lay across the thwart trembling and gasping for breath, my heart pounding like a hammer. I lifted my arm and waved to the raft, now two hundred yards away, then slowly I untied the paddle from the sail and paddled back to the raft; it took nearly half an hour. The long shapes of two sharks circled curiously twenty feet down; they must have had breakfast.

Lyn had been sitting against the central thwart trying to rest after her watch and the following is her account of what happened in the raft after Douglas shouted, 'Dad, the dinghy's gone.'

I saw Dougal's body hurtle past me as he dived into the sea. The silence was broken by the cry of 'Shark' from Douglas, followed by a despairing shriek from Neil, 'Daddy! Daddy!' We all crowded to see past Douglas blocking the doorway. Dougal was cutting through the water faster than *Ednamair* was sailing and could not have kept up such a speed for more than a few minutes. The shark was close behind him to his right and his feet were threshing the water in a racing crawl. 'I can't see him,' I said, 'he's gone.' The raft had slewed round in the swell and we had lost sight of him. 'Don't panic! Don't panic!' Robin shouted. Then Douglas cried, 'He's done it! He's made it!' 'Good old Dad,' this from Sandy. Only Douglas could see him now and he gave us a running commentary. 'He's taking the sail down now, it's down, he's getting the paddle off the sail.' Douglas craned his neck to see as the raft slewed round more, and we scrambled over the thwart to the aft compartment to look through the back door. There, miraculously, we saw him, the dinghy like a cockleshell on the crest of a wave with Dougal paddling furiously, first one side then the other with such a look of concentration and determination on his haggard face. Relief flooded through me and I heard myself singing 'There goes my love', that wonderful song from *Dr Zhivago*. It was a long time before he reached us and as he fell through the doorway into the bottom of the raft, his face grey with exhaustion, I pressed the sipper jar to his lips. He shook his head but I made him drink, then I put a piece of glucose in his mouth, cradling his head in my arms until his strength returned, and shuddering as I thought of how lonely and desperate we had felt cut off from our only hope for survival, *Ednamair* and my beloved Dougal.

On my return to the raft we tested the wire and found it frayed under the plastic in two places, broke it, rejoined it and in doing so, made it short enough to fasten a large nylon rope between the raft and the dinghy as a reserve, after which we rigged up a sea anchor which would automatically trip if the *Ednamair* broke away from the raft again, and stop her from sailing away. We had not only closed the stable door this time, we'd hobbled the horse as well! I didn't relish a repeat performance of that swim; not ever.

There was quite a lot of rain water in the bottom of the dinghy, mixed with some turtle blood from the sail and some sea water which I had spilled into the dinghy after my swim. As it was unpalatable we decided to use it by introducing it into our bodies by enema so that it could be absorbed through the rectal membrane and intestinal wall into the bloodstream. Douglas stripped a piece of rubber tubing from the raft ladder and I tapered the end with a scalpel blade, fashioning it into a makeshift enema tube. This was joined to the long bellows tube and Lyn made a funnel for the top from a polythene bag. Lyn expertly administered enemas to myself, Douglas, the twins, then herself (I poured the water in) in that order. Robin declined the enema. I looked at Lyn and she said it didn't matter yet. The idea this time was not so much to promote bowel movement as to allow us to absorb water which would be otherwise undrinkable. In the undulating raft it was a hilarious and undignified procedure requiring a steady hand and a lot of patience but we managed without spilling too much. We took between a pint and two pints each, which with our shrunken stomachs was more than we had been able to drink.

Our noon position of 5°15′ North and 250 miles west of Espinosa put us inside the official limits of the Doldrums; we had made the rain area in fifteen days. I solemnly reflected that if we had stayed at sea anchor where *Lucette* sank and hoped for rescue, we should have been dead by now. We had travelled about four hundred miles, about seven hundred to go, and had as much, if not more, food and water than when we started. Our condition was much worse it was true, but I hoped that the increase in our water supply would help to put that right; we could not hope for an improvement otherwise until we left the raft. I still had strong misgivings about our ability to fit into *Ednamair* along with the necessary equipment. We had had only about six inches of freeboard when we had been all aboard in the Galapagos; six inches wasn't much in the middle of the Pacific with sharks about, and even if I managed to save flotation pieces from the raft it would be very difficult to support the dinghy with them. We couldn't afford to be swamped, not even once, for our water and stores would be ruined even if we saved ourselves.

As I listed in my thoughts the items we required to take into the dinghy with us, my mind boggled at the thought of trying to fit us in as well, so I stopped thinking about it and decided to start immediately on a propaganda campaign concerning the absolute necessity for instant obedience when we took to the dinghy in order to keep the correct trim. Rain had begun falling again and it settled to a steady downpour throughout the night. We would need a canopy over the dinghy to keep the rain out rather than catch it if this was the sort of weather we could expect. I was glad the Ancient Mariner was wrong, just the same!

### Sixteenth day

The rain continued all night long, and as we bailed the warm sea water out of the raft we were glad not to be spending this night in the dinghy at least. I went over to the dinghy twice in the night to bail out, for the rain was filling her quite quickly, and I shivered at the low temperature of the rain water. The raft canopy offered grateful warmth when I returned, and the puddles of salt water in the bottom of the raft seemed less hostile after the chill of the dinghy. We all huddled together on top of the flotation chambers, our legs and bottoms in the water and although we did not sleep, we rested, for the work of blowing and bailing now went on around the clock, the bailer passing back and forth between the two compartments. Our sores stung as we knocked them against the raft and each other, our eyes were suppurating, our limbs permanently wrinkled and lumpy with boils, my backside was badly blistered from sunburn acquired on my turtle dressing expeditions, which made it necessary for me to lie on my tummy all the time, a painful piece of carelessness.

The rain continued to beat on the calm sea till mid-morning, when after a few desultory bursts of sunshine, the weather closed in again and it drizzled for the rest of the day. I had decided to postpone the evacuation of the raft until the weather improved a little and I detected a feeling of relief amongst the others. (It wasn't until much later that I learned that my propaganda about trim had been so effective that they were frightened to go into the dinghy at all!) We had enough problems without adding cold to them so we ate our dried turtle and fish, drinking plenty of water with it and feeling much better for it.

We had made no progress in the windless weather so I entered our noon position the same as the day before and during the afternoon we talked at length about what we should have to do when the time came to get into the dinghy, which pieces of the raft we would cut out and which pieces of essential equipment we would take, and where they would be stowed. As evening closed in the drizzle eased a little and the air became much warmer. We bailed and blew in the darkness until Douglas suddenly said, 'Quiet!' We listened, holding our breath. 'Engines,' he whispered. I could hear the faint beat of what might have been a propeller blade; it grew louder. I climbed into the dinghy with a torch but could neither see nor hear anything from there. I flashed SOS around the horizon in all directions for a couple of minutes but there was no answering light, and after a further round of flashes returned to the raft. We speculated on the possibility of its being a submarine bound for the atomic testing grounds at Tahiti where a test was shortly to take place, and then took it a little further and wondered what spy submarine would pick up survivors and if it did, what then?

The twins talked quietly in a corner about the sort of cat they were going to have when we returned to England, where they would keep it and what they would feed it on, and how they would house train it. Neil loved furry animals and could talk for hours on the subject. Douglas was back on roast rabbit and Robin was in rhapsodies over oatmeal porridge and milk. Lyn and I thanked our destinies for water, it was so good!

That night will live in our memories as one of utter misery. Our mouths were raw with the rough surface of the bellows tube, our lungs and cheeks ached with the effort of keeping the raft inflated. Because of the sea water on the floor of the raft we tried to lie with our bodies on top of the flotation chambers, and because we lay on the flotation chambers we squeezed the air out of them more quickly. Lyn was terrified in case one of the twins should fall asleep face downwards in the after compartment and drown, for we now bailed only in the forward section, and even then we could not bail quickly enough to keep it dry; the after section was flooded to a depth of three inches. I estimated that we could probably keep the raft afloat for a few days more, but the effort involved was depriving us of all bodily stamina, our limbs, almost hourly, suffered extensions of boil-infested areas, and we were pouring our lives away in this struggle to keep afloat. Our evacuation to the dinghy had to come, and soon; death in the dinghy would come as a result of an error of judgement, a capsize perhaps, or through being swamped in heavy weather; either of these in my estimate was preferable to the deterioration of our physical and mental state, through sheer exhaustion, into submission and death.

### Seventeenth day

The rain stopped in the early morning before daybreak and as the first rays of sun reached into the raft, probing our livid skin eruptions with warming fingers of light, I announced that I hoped to transfer to the dinghy today. I didn't expect a wave of enthusiastic support but I was a bit disappointed by the absence of any display of interest and surprised myself by asking the others if they wanted to stay on in the raft. Every morning they had declared they couldn't stand another night like the last one, but this morning it was different; this morning, last night *was* the last one and the unknown suddenly yawned ahead. Robin demurred and said he was prepared to manage a few days longer, Lyn worried about cramped conditions and trim, Sandy wanted to go, Neil didn't really care, he was hungry, and Douglas wondered if we wouldn't be swamped if the seas worsened. They left it to me in the end so I said, 'Right, the dinghy it is.'

I set Douglas to cutting away the door pieces on the raft for capes to shield us from rain and after preparing a small canopy, went over to *Ednamair* to fit it over the bow to shed spray. I bailed out the rain water first then transferred the foot of the sail to the bow so that she would ride stern to the raft, and fastened the towropes with a strop to the stern. Then I cleared the decks. Over went the turtle shells, laboriously scraped and cleaned. Then the lifejackets; I had given them careful thought, they were of kapok, saturated with water and weighed about forty pounds each, they wouldn't help us to keep afloat but it was just conceivable that they might help to sink us, so over they went. Various other trophies followed, then the pieces of wood and lumps of metal that had been saved simply because they were there; empty flare cases, turtle flippers and the canvas cover for the raft, a bulky lump of uselessness. Douglas was now cutting away all the useful pieces of rope from the raft and they were collected and stowed in the onion bag. I fitted the bow canopy then returned to the raft. The twins went over to *Ednamair*, their young agile bodies balancing easily. Then Lyn and Robin struggled into the tiny dinghy with fearful anticipation of disaster; Douglas and I remained to begin the demolition in earnest.

We cut off the double canopy first, passing it over to the dinghy, then scissors and knife making quick work of the worn fabric we hacked off a canopy arch support to use as a flotation collar. The other ripped badly as we cut the canopy from it. Then the grab lines were saved from around the raft, as were the rope ladders and other lines. To our surprise, a turtle poked its head up to view the proceedings so we caught it, slipped a rope around its flippers and passed it over to Robin to hold until we could deal with it; no point in passing up good food just because we were moving house. I accidentally sliced into one of the float chambers and had to hold the cut together to keep us afloat until Douglas had passed all the loose material

across to *Ednamair*. We cut out the central thwart which had
a double skinned flotation chamber, then as the floor of the
raft tilted steeply downwards I saw, too late, the scissors slide
through the hole at the edge of the floor and disappear into
the depths. Douglas went aboard the dinghy while I cut away
the remaining useful pieces with the knife. The whole raft had
now collapsed except for the forward floor piece which, though
inflated, leaked rather badly and would go down in about half
an hour. Waist deep in water I made my way to the dinghy,
climbed aboard and shoved the remains of the raft away; it
would sink in a short space of time when it had lost enough
buoyancy. We had cast off the towing wire to sink with the
raft but kept the nylon painter.

We all stared in silence at what was left of the raft as we
drifted away from its sinking remnants. It had served us well
and now, as its bits floated around us, we felt touched with
sorrow at its passing, for when it was gone there would be
nothing but the sea to look at. Good old Siggy, his gift had
been our haven for over two weeks and the pieces left over
would still serve us in times of need. I turned my attention
back to the dinghy.

The twins had settled happily in their places in the bow,
Lyn and Robin sat on the centre thwart one on each side of
the mast, and Douglas and I in the stern. We took the sail
down and streamed the sea anchor to bring *Ednamair* bow on
to the waves while we dealt with the turtle. With a heave,
Douglas and I lifted the turtle over the stern of the dinghy
and secured its thrashing flippers and vicious beak. So far so
good. We were keeping good trim, and even with the extra
weight of the turtle aboard, *Ednamair* rode the waves without
shipping any water. Admittedly the waves weren't very big but
it was an encouraging start.

The rest of *Ednamair*'s crew had not yet been privileged to
witness my expertise with a butcher's knife, and I set to work
to put this omission to rights. The knife had more the appearance of a saw than a sharp blade and while I managed to sever
the arteries and catch the blood without spilling much, it took
a long time for me to hack through the tough belly shell. We
indulged in our usual blood imbibing orgy (Robin had become
quite partial to it and had two cupfuls), then ate some of the

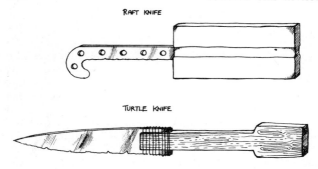

Tools of the trade: turtle knife consisted of broken blade of kitchen knife with an improvised handle

steak for lunch and started to clear up the boat, sorting out the jumbled pieces of canopy and rope, pieces of sail, spare sea anchor, rain capes and stores. The flotation pieces were lashed alongside ready to be secured in position when we had prepared the lashings.

Our noon position at 5°20′ North 250 miles west of Cape Espinosa (95°30′W) demonstrated how little wind we had experienced in the last few days. The sea was very calm now and I had decided to try to sail bow first, steering with an oar, to make as much easting as possible in the quiet seas. When the waves became too high for comfort we could always change the sail around to the stern again and sail stern first, presenting the more seaworthy part of the dinghy to the weather. While I made and secured a grommet to the rudder pins to house the steering oar, Douglas and Robin slung the pieces of turtle meat from the rigging to dry and Lyn and the twins were busy stowing the stores and finding places for the smaller pieces of equipment; we were all careful not to move our weight to the opposite side of the dinghy without first warning everyone that the move was about to take place, and arranging for a body on the other side of the boat to move across simultaneously in the opposite direction in order to maintain an even keel. In fact, the dinghy was more stable, with all the bottom weight lowering her centre of gravity, than I had imagined she would be.

The day remained overcast and we were spared the necessity

of rigging a sun canopy until later in the afternoon, so I concentrated on securing the flotation collar round the bow, lashing the ends of the long, sausage-like float to the leeboard fittings and then lifting the centre of the sleeve just under the gunwhale at the bows so that if the dinghy plunged its bow into a sea, the collar would not only support it but would prevent any waves breaking into the dinghy from ahead. The other float (the central thwart from the raft) was lashed across the dinghy behind the central thwart and used as a back rest for those seated there.

We now had more room to move around so with Douglas balancing for me, I moved to the bows and rigged the canopy over the forestay, covering the dinghy from the centre thwart forward to the bows and lashing the sides of the canopy to the gunwhales rather in the form of a tent, under which the twins at least would have some shelter. Most of the smaller pieces of equipment found a home in the bows, while the water cans, cups and bailers were kept under the stern seat. The box containing the dried fish and meat was placed on the bottom of the dinghy abaft the central thwart. The twins tucked their small bodies under the canopy in the bow, Lyn and Robin distributed themselves one each side of the dried stores box and Douglas and I sat on the thwart, leaning back on the float. As night fell, we tried to find comfort for our suppurating limbs, but whichever way we turned the unyielding wood and fibreglass gave no ease.

There were also some compensations, no blowing up to do except an occasional puff at the float; no bailing, for the sea was calm, and no assaults in the rear from the predatory dorado; our posteriors protected by the fibreglass had gained a little peace if they had lost some comfort! In the arc of the cloud-strewn sky the stars twinkled down where before we had had only the raft canopy to look at, the roof of the cave that had protected us from the loneliness of the ocean. Now, for us as for the far-ranging albatross and petrels, the sky was our roof, the ocean our larder and the wind our power, though at present there was so little of it that we left *Ednamair* idling at her sea anchor for the night.

Galapagos Storm Petrel (Mother Carey's Chicken)

### *Eighteenth day*

The night sky cleared and daybreak brought a beautiful sunrise. One flying fish had landed in the dinghy during the night and this was sliced up and mixed with some fresh turtle meat and the meat juices collected in the piece of sail in which some of the meat was wrapped. Together with some pieces of turtle fat, it made a very tasty dish.

A slight drizzle had occurred in the early hours so that the meat which festooned the rigging hung in limp damp strips, and some of it still uncured from the second turtle had started to go bad. It didn't go offensively bad and stinking (at least we didn't smell it!), but simply disintegrated into a rather slimy mess. There were, of course, no insects around to assist the process of decomposition although we did observe a type of water spider which skated on the surface of the sea in calm weather. We had the constant companionship of the storm petrels, those delightful little birds which flit endlessly over the ocean, dipping their feet into the surface of the sea while picking up food (pieces of turtle fat which we threw to them), earning themselves the South American name of 'walkers on the water' and the British sailors' fond nickname of 'Mother Carey's chickens'. Majestic frigate birds, too, soared across the sky at intervals often working in pairs to catch flying fish, especially in cloudy, rainy weather. The flying fish seem to shoal in this type of weather and it is not uncommon to see a frigate bird

Frigate Bird

Blue-footed Booby

dive down menacingly at a shoal of flying fish, frightening
them into flight in the direction of its partner, waiting to pick
them off. Flying fish, taking to the air when attacked by dorado,
are likewise often picked up by a swooping frigate bird before
they can regain the water and on one occasion we saw a frigate
bird and a dorado collide in mid-air, both in pursuit of the
same flying fish! The frigate birds, like the storm petrels, seem
to remain in flight over the ocean, and are spectacular hunters
with their hawk-like strikes at their prey.

A new arrival in the way of bird life came on this, our first
morning in the dinghy; a blue-footed booby circled us curiously
and landed in the sea not far away. It preened its feathers and
surveyed us with the rather comical expression peculiar to
these birds. I caught my breath, then shouted as I saw a shark
nosing upwards towards the bird; the booby looked at me
curiously, then sensing the presence of danger, stuck its head
under the water. The shark, now only a few feet away, moved
swiftly towards it, but to my surprise the booby, instead of

taking off, pecked at the shark's nose three or four times, then as the shark turned away, spread its wings and flew off. The shark was young and perhaps just curious, but I wondered how the booby would have fared if it had been an older and hungrier shark.

It had been cold in the night without the shelter from the canopy and we were grateful for the warming sun. After sorting out the meat, discarding the slimy pieces (even the scavenger fish were not interested in them!), we pulled the sea anchor aboard and set the sail, sheeted to the bow. The light southerly breeze allowed us to steer north-east, using the steering oar to hold the dinghy on course; we were on our way again, and with six hundred miles to go, we were nearly half way to the coast!

Douglas and I had changed places with Lyn and Robin, a precarious business involving much bad language on my part and fearful reaction on theirs, the tiny dinghy tipping dangerously as frantic yells of 'Trim!' rent the Pacific air. The change was necessary to allow Douglas and me to steer, for neither Lyn nor Robin could use the steering oar or find the direction in which to steer, and although Douglas could scull expertly this was the first time he had used the oar as a rudder.

As we settled down again, the dinghy only making half a knot in the slight breeze, we talked of the North Staffordshire countryside where Lyn and the children had been born, of rolling hills and valleys in the Peak district. It was at this time that we started talking of the thing that was eventually to become our main topic of conversation: a kitchen-type restaurant in the North Staffordshire town of Leek, to be called Dougal's Kitchen. It was a wonderful opportunity to talk about food.

Our estimated noon position was 5°30′ North, 245 miles west of Cape Espinosa; we had made our first easting since *Lucette* had sunk and I felt that we were now far enough north to allow some set and drift for the counter current which runs east through the Doldrums; we really were on our way home!

The sores and boils on our limbs had already begun to dry and while they were still badly inflamed and septic, the surrounding skin felt much better and there was no further extension of the infected areas. Our clothes had begun to disintegrate rapidly now, and our principal concern was to avoid

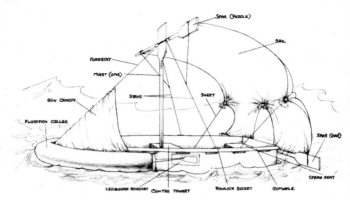

*Ednamair* under way

being sunburned on hitherto unexposed parts of our bodies (my contortions to avoid putting pressure on my blistered posterior were sufficient warning to the others); it was the warmth these clothes afforded us at night that concerned us, far more than any moral aspect. Indeed our absence of clothing was never discussed in terms of morality and while the capes that had been cut from the doors of the raft saved us many a night of misery by containing a little of our body warmth, we never wore them during the day unless it rained, our singlets or shirts affording adequate cover from the sun while we exposed the various parts of our distressed anatomy to the dry fresh air.

We steered a steady north-easterly course all day and then towards evening the wind freshened a little, building the waves big enough to slop in over the square stern of the dinghy, so with much manoeuvring to maintain an even keel, the steering oar was lashed across the stern, the sail brought aft and sheeted to the two ends of the oar. This move allowed the dinghy to ride bow on to the waves again and we proceeded more slowly, stern first, but the danger of being swamped by a wave was much lessened. Steering in this position was done by means of pulling the sail down on the side the stern was required to move towards, and we were able to angle the dinghy across the wind by as much as forty-five degrees, if the sea was not

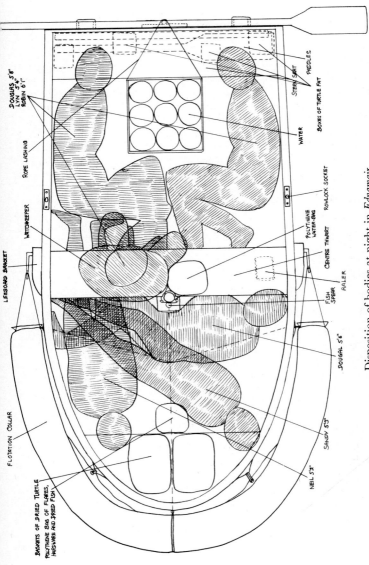

Disposition of bodies at night in *Ednamair*

Labels (clockwise from top right):
PADDLES
STERN SEAT
BOXES OF TURTLE FAT
WATER
ROWLOCK SOCKET
POLYTHENE WATER-BAG
CENTRE THWART
BAILER
FISH SPEAR
DOUGAL 5'6"
SANDY 5'3"
NEIL 5'1"
BASKETS OF DRIED TURTLE
POLYTHENE BAG OF FLARES, HARDWARE AND DRIED FISH
FLOTATION COLLAR
LEEBOARD SOCKET
WATCHKEEPER
ROPE LASHING
DOUGLAS 5'6"
LYN 5'4"
ROBIN 6'1"

too rough, by this method. The fore and aft trim was of much importance now for if the bow was too light it tended to fall away from the wind bringing the dinghy broadside to the waves, a most vulnerable position; so I streamed the sea anchor from the bow and left it half-tripped so that it would not hinder our progress too much while keeping the bow pointed to the waves. We also moved the two persons from the back seat into the bottom of the dinghy to give it more forward trim. With the sea anchor streamed we found we could lash the sail in position, making *Ednamair* self-steering and allowing us to continue watches as before, but now Lyn insisted that I be spared the necessity of taking a watch at all for I was liable to be called out at all times and the heavy work of tending rigging and turtle dressing was most onerous in my exhausted condition. (Douglas was quite eager to take his share in dressing turtles but he is heavy-handed and I dared not risk breaking the knife again.)

The night closed in on *Ednamair*, a lonely speck in the vast reaches of the ocean, and as we arranged and rearranged our comfortless limbs we felt that we had conquered a major obstacle to our survival. We could manage to live in the dinghy.

### Nineteenth day

Rain showers in the night caused us some discomfort and the watchkeeper bailed as we tried to keep dry under the waterproof canopy which we had stretched partially across the stern (it wasn't quite wide enough to reach all the way over), but the twins under the bow canopy managed to stay fairly warm and dry. We used our rain capes of course at night in order to retain body warmth though they weren't much use at keeping us dry in the open thwarts.

Cloud increased again during the early morning watches, with lightning in the distance, and more continuous rain fell at daybreak. The weather was cold and the wind had increased to a fresh east-south-easterly breeze, so we streamed the sea anchor full open, reefed in the sail and set about collecting some rain water. Our minds clung to our old-established lines of behaviour, for we stretched out the old canopy, bringing it

Young Booby

over our heads with the pipe leading down from the hollow in the centre to where we filled the empty tins in the bottom of the boat. We held out the canopy with arms aching, to extend the catchment area, and suffered while the rain water slowly trickled into the empty tins. It still tasted of rubber but the yellow dye seemed finally to have washed off. We all gained a certain amount of shelter from this method of collection but it was certainly bought at the price of aching limbs and short tempers, for the cans wobbled precariously on the sloping bottom of the dinghy and more than one was knocked over by an unexpected movement of the canopy and spilled its contents into the bottom of the dinghy.

The turtle meat was giving us much cause for concern, for while that which was already dried and stored in the box had a slight covering of mould, the continuously damp atmosphere caused the hanging meat to sweat and we feared that our last two turtles would be of no use as dry stores. We therefore ate more of the fresh turtle meat than usual, saving our dry stores as much as possible. The rain helped in some degree to keep the seas from building up to dangerous proportions and of course, we were keeping our containers and our bellies full. The relief of not having to worry about water was compensation enough for the meat problem.

The rain cleared after midday and towards two o'clock another blue-footed booby (a young one this time) circled the dinghy and landed in the water, inspecting our strange appearance, then deciding we were harmless enough it flew round us again, and swooped down, folding its five foot wingspan to land on Douglas's shoulder as he sat in the stern of the dinghy. Douglas, looking a bit like Long John Silver, glanced sideways at the four-inch razor sharp beak two inches from his right eye and hastily averted his eye in case it pecked at him. The bird seemed quite unafraid and while we admired its beautiful plumage and streamlined appearance we could not help our thoughts turning to this alternative source of food. I told what I knew about seabirds, that they were salty, stringy and full of lice. Having agreed that only in an extreme emergency would we consider these birds as a source of food a small voice piped up from the bow, 'Pluck it, I'll eat it!' We turned in astonishment to Neil, the source of this comment and assured him that he could have some turtle meat if he was hungry. It seemed that we adults were slower to adjust after all!

Intermittent rain continued in the afternoon; the seas were smoothed by the rain so we half-tripped the sea anchor, unreefed the sail and resumed our northerly course. The swells, still fifteen feet high and dangerous to our small freeboard, put us in a position where there was no alternative to caution; a second chance after being swamped would be a meagre one indeed, for all our stores and fresh water would be ruined, to say nothing of the probable loss of life from shark attack. (Anything which struggles and splashes on the surface can attract and stimulate attacks by sharks.) I had been considering the usefulness of the float as a backrest for the central thwart, and its drawbacks as an obstacle when we changed positions. We decided that it would be better if it was not in the dinghy at all, so we pulled in the sea anchor, attached the float to it and then streamed it again, with the float now lying in our wake to mark the sea anchor's position. We all agreed the increased room was worth the loss in comfort. The evening brought a glorious rainbow and we gazed spellbound at the riot of colour which suffused sky, sea and the dispersing clouds into the brilliant pattern of a Pacific sunset.

### Twentieth day

We all remembered Lyn's birthday. The Robertson family sometimes think that America chose to be independent on July the fourth for that particular reason. Dear Lyn, she had so much to put up with from us all, especially me, and she bore it with great fortitude.

We caught another turtle in the morning. It was a female but, alas, it had no eggs; it brought fresh meat to the birthday menu, however, and dressing and carving it occupied our morning. We all chewed the turtle bones at lunch and especially enjoyed the flavour of old dried turtle meat marinated in the fresh meat juices. With dried dorado strips as well as fresh steak, we feasted, and drank our fill of water to celebrate.

Our estimated noon position of 5°55′ North and still 245 miles west of Cape Espinosa was a cautious estimate on my part, for we had made some westing the day before which absorbed the easterly drift of the current. *Ednamair* still rode to the sea anchor and float as we waited patiently for the seas to subside.

We rested quietly in the afternoon, and talked of all the nice things we had had on previous birthdays. After a long-drawn-out birthday tea, thirty minutes of slow chewing and sipping water, we sang 'Happy Birthday'. It sounded a bit odd in a small boat in the middle of the Pacific but it did our morale good, so as the quiet of the evening drew in we sang lots of songs; Robin sang Welsh ones, I sang Scots ones and Lyn sang English ones. In the now peaceful atmosphere of the Pacific sunset our voices carried well so that for the moment I felt almost at one with this environment, that we could go on, not simply surviving, but creating a way of life that had no other objective than life on the sea, from the sea. It came as something of a shock when I realised that the twins, although they had joined in the songs they knew, might be afraid that this was in fact happening, that we would go on living in this way for months to come.

I decided that it would be good for them to see our progress towards the coast so I showed them where we were on my chart and when we could expect to reach land. We all talked at some length of the speed we might make and when I mentioned that when we were close enough, say about two hundred miles, we'd have to start rowing at night for we would lose the current, it sounded as if we were nearly there. I tried to make thirty-five days sound less than a month when Douglas asked for an estimate of how long it would take us to get there, but one of the most dangerous of all the attitudes we could adopt was that it would be easy or that the sea was our friend. I knew from hard-won experience that where the land may be kindly to man, the sea was as impartial as the sky and that, in an environment where every other living creature had adapted and perfected its means of survival over millions of years, our chances of surviving amongst them lay in our ability to adapt our past experience to present circumstances. Our ability to fashion tools, to help each other physically and psychologically and to use knowledge as a weapon of offence as well as defence, these were the attributes that would allow us to live from the sea.

That we could live from the sea had become not just a possibility but a fact. 'We must get these boys to land' Lyn had said in the beginning: we would do just that. I knew it now for the first time, and the knowledge came like a release from physical pain. I looked across the centre thwart to Lyn, crouched awkwardly in the bow, each arm round a twin, wondering if I could share this revelation as a birthday present, and as she looked back into my eyes, I not only saw the love shining from them, but also the intuitive knowledge that my message had been received. After nearly twenty years of marriage she could still surprise me; indeed I felt she had known it all along and that it was I who had just got the message!

The watches for the night were set as twilight deepened and the dorado flashed iridescent under the *Ednamair* in their endless pursuit of food. These big fish posed one of the knottiest problems of our existence; how to get them from their present location into the dinghy, only a matter of a few feet but a mile of expertise away, was becoming an obsession in my resting hours. I knew the spear I had made was only strong enough for the smallest of the dorado and we seldom saw them at all, far less came within striking distance of them. Robin stirred uneasily in his sleep, then suddenly he sat up and yelled 'Where's the spike? We won't have any water left if we can't find it!' Douglas on watch looked closely at him. 'He's still asleep. It's alright Robin,' he soothed. Robin lay back and twisting his long legs into another position kicked Neil, pulled the sail cover off Lyn and jabbed his bony knees into my back. 'Ye gods!' I groaned and thumped his offending knees with my fist; they moved with alacrity, kicked Neil again, then as he turned over he dragged the rubber canopy sheet off the rest of us and thrust the food box at an angle into Lyn's chest. 'Robin!' we all shouted out. It was fifteen minutes before we settled down again sorted out in our separate and several spaces and since fifteen minutes was about the maximum length of time we could suffer the impact of the fibreglass on our sparsely covered bones and boils, it was time for Robin to move again.

### Twenty-first day

The clear night gave way to cloudy squally weather as the dawn approached, and in the early daylight hours *Ednamair* tugged impatiently at the float and sea anchor streamed to windward of her. We shared the flying fish, which had come aboard in Robin's watch, for breakfast, along with some turtle meat. As we put away the water jar, the dinghy yawed sharply and Lyn pointed, with an urgent cry, to the float drifting a hundred yards away from us; the sea anchor rope had broken! We quickly downed the sail and at first tried to paddle back to the bright yellow float. One of the paddles broke, so we quickly substituted the oar to which the sail had been lashed and clearing the centre thwart Douglas, our champion oarsman, set to row with oar and paddle, an unequal combination to use in the unequal contest of overloaded boat against wind and weather. Our other oar was rigged as the mast and would cause much loss of time and chaos if taken down so Douglas set grimly to work, his wasted muscles bunched like whipcord as he thrust the dinghy forward with powerful strokes. Fifteen minutes passed and he still rowed with steady rhythm, gaining foot by foot against the buffeting waves. His breath came in harsh gasps now as I encouraged him with 'You're doing fine Doug, we're half way'. The float was still nearly a hundred yards away so I started giving him the yardage to go, eighty, sixty, and so on, and though I could see that the effort was becoming an endurance test, he steadfastly refused to give in. Gradually we drew closer until at last, after thirty-five minutes, I was able to secure the broken rope to the eyebolt in the bow of the dinghy. Douglas sat gasping for breath on the centre thwart and Lyn hastily passed him some water and a piece of glucose from the rations. I knew that even with an oar apiece, Robin and I could not have done it between us and that only Douglas's constant rowing practice (it was his favourite form of exercise) had made it possible. It was a salutary lesson to us too, in demonstrating how difficult it would be to retrieve anybody or anything lost overboard in rough weather, particularly the paddle, for that would mean dismantling the mast before we could start! Douglas had demonstrated that he was still in fairly good condition and I felt cheered by the fact that when the time came to row in calm weather, we would be able to do it.

Our noon position, 6° North and 240 miles west of Cape Espinosa, gave us all a boost, for our eastward drift had now begun on paper as well as in fact (I hoped). I spent some time making a rope strong enough to hold the sea anchor and float for we were running short of suitable material which would withstand the constant chafing to which the sea anchor rope was subjected. The boys settled down to a game of Twenty Questions, which was followed by Robin telling of his travels across Yugoslavia and Greece while Lyn sewed diligently at our tattered clothing.

The afternoon was overcast but dry, and the turtle meat now looked as if it could be saved if some more dry weather followed on the morrow. As we gathered in the drier pieces before night fell, Douglas cried 'A flare!' We scrambled to look, with our usual cries of 'Trim her!' as *Ednamair* tilted dangerously to one side. I didn't see it, and Lyn wasn't sure, but Douglas assured me that he had seen a green flare, a signal often given by a submarine on manoeuvres, and that he'd seen it go up as well as down (falling stars don't go up!) We scanned the sea closely in the deepening twilight but we could see nothing. I brought out the torch and signalled in the appropriate direction but I felt that the sacrifice of one of our three remaining hand flares was unjustified, particularly if the submarine had merely surfaced to periscope depth and might not even be on our side of the horizon. We could hear no engines even though we pressed our ears to the hull of *Ednamair*, so I decided to wait, and if no further signs of its presence were seen, to write it off as another miss. We were almost casual in our acceptance of this disappointment, to me a healthy sign that our thoughts were no longer centred on rescue as our main hope.

The sea had quietened again with the lull of evening and we were no longer shipping any water as the waves slopped along the small freeboard of *Ednamair*'s hull, relieving us of the need to bail. We still enjoyed the relaxation from the effort to keep the raft inflated and our hurt limbs were no longer so inflamed and painful.

### Twenty-second day

After a quieter night, during which I slept for three hours, a most extraordinarily long time for me these days, my usual period of slumber lasting no longer than an hour at most (Lyn, like me, slept little, but the boys slept whenever time and comfort allowed), the still hours of dawn brought another turtle. The usual frenzied scramble ensued, both to clear enough space to bring it aboard and to arrange ourselves in the proper places to perform the operation. Sandy decided that he wanted to help this time, so Lyn went into the bows with Neil. With everyone in position the turtle, a big one this time, was pulled to the side, beak snapping and clawed flippers waving wildly, then Douglas and I turned it on its back and slid it aboard while Robin and Sandy trimmed the boat from the other side. Sucker fish, one nine inches long, dropped from the under belly of the turtle and flapped wildly in the bottom of the dinghy and though we had caught no fresh flying fish that morning, none of us

9-inch Remora or Sucker Fish

could bring ourselves to eat the grey, jellified flesh of these sucker fish.

I had made a handle for the broken knife blade and could now impose a better control on the cutting edge; it nevertheless took some effort and perseverance to find the artery in the maze of tough tendons which abound in a turtle's sinewy neck area, and the lacerating claws took their toll as we worked in the confined space. Eventually the artery was severed and with the blood spurting into containers held ready, we drank our fill although Lyn and the twins were less eager for it now that water was more plentiful. Robin was our champion vampire at three full cups.

The business of cutting open the heavy shell and the careful incisions against the inside of the outer shell to extract the meat was heavy and exacting work. Many times I cut into my own numb fingers instead of the turtle. Douglas now helped me by putting his strong arms to use, levering the shell and pulling the joints this way and that to enable me to cut in at the awkward places. It was a female again, and this time our expectation of eggs was met in full by a golden harvest of over a hundred yolks. After the eggs had been gathered into a bag, Sandy collected the deep yellow fat, which lined the shell, into containers for processing for oil later. It was the largest turtle we had caught so far and we probably had twenty-five pounds of steak and bone from it, as well as eggs and fat. Douglas struggled to extract the flipper bones, an arduous task, using the blunt raft knife, the blade of which had already broken against the mast.

As soon as the meat and fat had been extracted the shell and offal were dumped overboard. We no longer worried about sharks for the dinghy was less vulnerable than the inflatable and we soon left the debris behind the dinghy, whereas the raft, being towed by the dinghy, had to pass over it. Sharks cruised around us almost continuously anyway and we had become used to seeing their stately progress with their attendant retinue of pilot fish in precise formation.

We prepared a veritable feast for lunch and with the juice from the meat we mixed in a dozen turtle eggs, then cutting up some mature dried turtle meat in small pieces we added it to the egg mixture. Fresh turtle meat and dried dorado were soused in this sauce (the last of the dorado alas) and after the meal we lay back, our stomachs feeling full for the second time since *Lucette* had been so violently taken from us. In fact, our stomachs had contracted so much that it now took very little to fill them; perhaps a blessing in disguise.

Our noon position estimated at 6°20′ North and 240 miles west of Cape Espinosa took into account a change of wind to the south-east, an unusual quarter for this area, and my fears were justified as the familiar cirrus stratus spread southwards from the northern sky. It seemed we were in for some foul weather so I checked the flotation collar fastenings and sea anchor ropes for fraying and also examined the knots. Synthetic fibre ropes have a tendency to resist knotting unless the ends are lashed with cord, and this was in very short supply, being used largely for hanging the drying food stocks.

We talked of Dougal's Kitchen in the afternoon, discussing recipes for the savoury pastries which were to be served with hot soup (of the old-fashioned home-made variety of course), in the colder months of the year. Not only did this subject allow us to talk about food but the site for such a restaurant allowed us to roam at will around the Leek district remembering all the vacant buildings and houses with nostalgic glee; the twins were particularly interested in this project, for nothing seemed more desirable to them than a beautiful hot Cornish pastie followed by large quantities of fruit and ice cream, consumed in the security of known surroundings. Robin, although he did not know Leek, was able to join in with his own recipes for good food and favourite dishes, and his knowledge of hotel and restaurant technique was most instructive.

The late afternoon brought squally conditions so the sail was reefed to ease the strain on the sea anchor ropes and with the

sea anchor now fully expanded we jerked uneasily at the end of
the anchor rope, plunging steeply in the short seas which broke
over the bow at times and sluiced into the dinghy in uncomfortable rather than dangerous quantities. We trimmed the
dinghy so that the bow would ride a little higher and shook out
the reef again so that we could steer *Ednamair* with the sail and
keep her bow pointing to any of the more dangerous waves, for
some of them were running across the wind in a most confused
fashion, catching us broadside on. At tea time the wind increased to a strong breeze and I took over the steering at four
o'clock, for the dinghy now yawed dangerously at times and we
all feared a capsize. The seas heightened as the evening
advanced and grimly we prepared for a rough night; the waves
were slopping aboard frequently now and the watchkeeper had
to bail almost continuously to clear the water from the bottom
of the dinghy. The rain came about eight o'clock and with the
wind swinging to the south, increased steadily in volume until by
ten o'clock a torrential downpour lashed us unceasingly. Both
Lyn and Robin bailed now and I peered anxiously into the
black night trying to spot the breaking waves so that I could
steer the bow into them, but occasionally a wave crest came at
us across the wind, catching *Ednamair* on the beam and slopping
a gallon or two of warm salt water into the boat amongst the
colder rain water. At eleven thirty the wind shifted again,
although the direction was difficult to determine, my only guide
being the long tradewind swell which still ran up from the
south-east, and this was visible only in the brilliant flashes of
lightning which illumined the sky at infrequent intervals.

I sat immobile, as animals do, trying to retain a small part of
dryness on my body by allowing the water to run off me in
established paths, but gradually as I moved to steer, and peer at
the sea, or the sail, I became saturated, it seemed, through the
layers of skin and flesh to my very bones.

### Twenty-third day

The torrential downpour kept up a steady drumming on the
sail and canopy, hissing loudly as it struck the sea around us;
the bailers scraped and splashed as they filled and emptied with
monotonous rhythm. Lyn and Robin, on their knees under

the waterproof sheet in the bottom of the boat, plied the bailers and Douglas tried to snatch some rest in the bow with the twins, but already the water had soaked them from underneath when a wave had broken into the boat, temporarily overwhelming the bailers. At half past one in the morning the wind eased slowly until the rain fell almost vertically. My particular burden became a little easier as the more frequent flashes of lightning allowed me to see where I was steering and the rain quickly flattened the breaking waves, so dangerous to our little craft, but the bailers' rhythmic beat scarcely altered as they emptied the rain water into the sea. At two o'clock the wind dropped completely and to our astonishment the rain doubled in intensity and grew colder until I wondered if we would have hailstones. The bailers now plied with increasing speed and I was so cold that I did not realise that the moaning noise I heard came from myself. Lightning hissed and flashed with increasing intensity and frequency and thunder pealed deafeningly in a continuous reverberation of sound. The rain doubled and redoubled until a frenzy of water fell from the sky; above the noise of the storm I could hear Sandy sobbing and Lyn praying while the bailers quickened their rhythm to try to keep pace with the torrent of water. Douglas now bailed as well while the twins held the bow canopy from spilling water into the boat. Like a statue, I sat, cold seeping through to my very brain, hands clutching the sail, ready to trim it the instant the next squall of wind struck. My eyes peered into the flashes of lightning to find the float marking the sea anchor. It was still ahead of us.

Lyn's voice rose above the tumult, coming from the darkness as if from another world. Quite distinctly I heard her say, 'Rub him, Robin!' and yet when I saw Robin in front of me, his arms stretched out towards me, I could feel nothing. Slowly he rubbed the feeling into my body, his warming hands rubbing at my back and ribs as I sat there until 'I'm alright now, Robin, thanks' I managed to shout above the noise of the rain. We were in cloudburst conditions now and there was no knowing what to expect next. It came like a hammer blow from behind us, the squall tore at the sail in my hand as I fought to control the dinghy, the rain suddenly lessened but the wavelets whipped up by the wind slopped over the stern, then the sea anchor held the bow and *Ednamair* swung to head into this new threat. 'Sing!'

shouted Douglas, 'Sing to keep warm' and burst into a wordless version of the Cuckoo Waltz. We sang everything from 'Those were the days, my friend' to 'God save the Queen' and from Beethoven's Ninth to the Twenty-third Psalm. The wind whipped the rain into my face and desperately I gathered the sail into the reefed position to prevent its being ripped to shreds. The wind-thrashed sail now added to the noise of the rain and thunder, and spume from the breaking waves, warmer than the rain, joined in the assault. The bailers hadn't managed to keep pace with the influx of water during the heaviest of the rain, particularly when Robin had stopped to succour me, but now they gained on it until the familiar scrape of the bailer on the bottom of the dinghy could be heard again. The rhythm slowed a little as the squall eased and the spray lessened. I released the sail and steered the yawing dinghy into the waves again. We were now stern on to the swell, a wind change of 180°; my mind filtered its knowledge of circular storms but I had never been in a storm centre like this one, it was almost like being caught in a giant water-spout. The rain had eased to a normal downpour again and grew slightly warmer; we were past the worst of it.

Dawn found us still bailing wearily, almost mechanically; occasionally a bailer would stop momentarily as the hand that held it relaxed in sleep, then scrape to life again in a half-remembered quickening of rhythm as it made up for lost time. I sat in the stern, rigid with cold, able only to move my arms to pull the sail this way and that as *Ednamair* yawed in the squally wind. At nine o'clock, Douglas, who had rested after the rain had eased, now relieved me at the helm and in a lull in the rain, Lyn and Robin pummelled my body back into feeling again. Gradually as the rain eased and the wind fell light, the bailers slowed and stopped; we slept as we knelt against the thwart, exhausted but still afloat, occasionally waking to clear the small amount of water in the bottom of the dinghy.

The rain still spotted the calm sea as we ate strips of dried turtle meat and a small portion of biscuit (a special treat) for breakfast. It was warmer now and as we huddled together under the sheet, Lyn told us she had counted seven people in *Ednamair* in the night, that she had had a vision of a presence rather than a person behind me, helping us to fight the storm. Although this was greeted with scepticism by Robin and Douglas, Lyn steadfastly maintained her belief in her vision, and indeed if this had helped her in the midst of that terrible storm, then it certainly had made a great contribution to our survival. We had been close to death many times in the night and the failure of any one of us to play our part could have meant destruction for us all. Twelve hours is a long time to be on the brink of eternity, and I wondered how much longer our weary bodies could have met the challenge.

As I lay down to rest I thought of that 180° change in the wind and what would have happened to a square-rigged ship, taken aback and probably dismasted in such a storm, then I dismissed the thought from my mind. They certainly couldn't have been any worse off than us!

Cloudy weather with intermittent rain continued throughout the day, the wind rising through squalls to a strong breeze, whipping wavetops to a creamy foam before the heavy showers beat the turbulent waters calm again. I estimated, or rather blindly guessed, at our position that noon as 6°50' North and 240 miles west of Cape Espinosa, for there had been many times in the night when our course and speed had been quite unknown to me.

Douglas steered throughout the day while the twins bailed, allowing Lyn, Robin and me to rest and as the afternoon progressed, dark threatening cloud again covered the northern sky and rolled towards us, bringing rain with the darkness, a moderate downpour by last night's standards, but heavy enough to keep Robin and me bailing like automatons (there was no wind so it was unnecessary to steer) while Lyn rubbed us warm. Douglas and the twins rested in the bows after their day's labour, and were soon asleep after our supper of dried turtle, the last of the eggs, and as much water as we wanted! (The twins also had their 'little supper' of emergency rations which Lyn prepared for them every night.)

### Twenty-fourth day

The steady scrape of the bailing cups went on through the night. Side by side, Robin and I knelt under the yellow sheet of raft canopy, our knees flattened against the fibreglass, our heads against the thwart as we threw the water over the side. The steady beat of the rain on our capes only served to lull our senses, and sleep, which would not come to my resting body, tried hard to take me unawares now. I felt Robin lean against me as he, too, dozed in exhausted slumber, then he would jerk awake again to the tyranny of the bailing cup. We could no longer feel any pain, our hands and limbs felt soaked to the bone, our skins were a crumpled mess of nerveless wrinkles, we shivered and bailed and sang songs, any songs, to keep our circulation going, and when we were too tired to sing, Lyn pummelled and rubbed our insensitive bodies to life again, but the scrape and splash of the bailing cups went on through the unrelenting downpour of rain, our hopes, our fears, our thirst, our despair, all forgotten in the emotionless limbo of anaesthesia by exhaustion.

Dawn came to us, a grey witness in the eastern sky; Robin was asleep as his kneeling body sagged sideways against the dinghy, the bailing cup still clutched in his hand, while Lyn knelt asleep against the stern seat, her body close to mine for warmth. My arm still moved in the motion of bailing until I realised that it had stopped raining and so sank into grateful oblivion. Death could have come to us too at this moment, without our knowledge or any resistance to its coming.

Douglas had taken over the steering as the southerly breeze strengthened during the morning. The rain still spotted and there was no sign of a break in the clouds yet. I awoke in mid-morning and checked the fastenings on the flotation collar, for one end had come adrift. While I seldom slept above an hour at any time, the boys suffered much from lack of sleep, their haggard faces belying their assurances that they were getting enough rest. We now ate without tasting our food, and drank water as an obligation to the dried turtle, rather than as a blessing from the sky. Our daydreams had switched from ice cream and fruit to hot stews, porridge, steak and kidney puddings, hotpots and casseroles. The dishes steamed fragrantly in our imaginations and as we described their smallest details to each other we almost tasted the succulent gravies as we chewed our meagre rations.

The dried meat was rapidly being used up since the hanging meat had grown a slimy film and was so unpalatable that I threw it overboard for fear of poisoning. Sickness of any descrip-tion was a hazard we could do well without; but it seemed that with the bountiful supply of fresh water, our appetites had grown, so rations of the dried turtle were severely reduced in case our larder should become empty before the next catch. The clouds thinned towards noon and the sun finally broke through in the early afternoon. We greeted him like a long-lost friend, almost as welcome as the rain had been a week before, and spread soaked items of equipment to dry on the thwarts. Most of the first-aid kit was ruined beyond salvation, and my log book, quite saturated, was spread carefully to dry.

At 7°40′ North, 230 miles west of Cape Espinosa (95°14′W) our noon position placed us approximately half way to land and we talked during the day of ways of beaching a boat, lighting fires without matches, jungle lore and Indians. Robin frightened the twins by telling them that there were cannibals on the wild coast of Nicaragua, where we might land. Their imaginations needed no stimulant to foment apprehension so Robin contritely reassured them of his joke. Douglas and Lyn had been talking about the possibility of making a net out of a piece of sail to catch plankton to reinforce our diet but it was decided to leave everything until the following day, for the sky had again darkened and we decided to snatch what rest we could in the day time if we were required to work all night. Our hearts sank as we prepared for another miserable night but the rain, when it came, was light and intermittent, almost a drizzle, requiring the services of one bailer and then only occasionally. Normal watches were resumed and we lay down to pass the night in dry discomfort, something of a luxury. The disposition of our bodies at night had found the most suitable arrangement to be Neil and Sandy lying lengthways in the bow with myself in a U-shape across the dingy just forward of the centre thwart. The water cans were transferred from under the stern seat into the big wooden box and this was kept lashed forward of the stern seat, allowing a sleeper to lie on each side of it (sideways only of course). The watchkeeper kept watch from the centre thwart, and all dry stores and food were kept under the bow canopy right forward where they were reasonably dry.

The fish and bird life had been little in evidence during the past two days although the dorado still weaved their patterns under the rain-spattered sea, but now with the advent of drier weather the sharks had returned and Lyn, taking the midnight watch, called me to deal with a large and frightening specimen which seemed intent on knocking the bottom out of the boat. I made contact with the business end of the fish spear on its next transit and it went off to seek a less spiteful playmate at a considerable rate of knots.

The rest of the night was peaceful enough, the rain having stopped before midnight and clearing skies giving the promise of a better day.

### Twenty-fifth day

Daylight brought sunshine and clear skies. A flying fish had landed on the canopy during Douglas's watch and he had made a good catch before it had time to slide off again. The twins had a half each for breakfast while we chewed a small piece of dried turtle meat; the larder was becoming too bare for comfort and we had just finished a discussion on whether it was better to eat up the remains of the dried turtle, and risk not catching any more, or whether to spin it out and risk it going bad in the damp weather, when a nicely sized female turtle popped its head up to have a good look at us. We cleared the space between the stern seat and the centre thwart, lifting the box of water cans on to the thwart, and then Neil came aft from the bow to do his share with this one. (He wasn't going to let Sandy be one up on him.)

The turtle bumped heavily against the bottom of the boat and tensely we waited to see if it would surface within reach. Douglas grabbed at the shell and I grappled with a back flipper, then we had its back against the side of the dinghy. 'Trim!' we shouted, and as we lifted the reptile inboard Neil and Robin leaned outwards on their side to counterbalance the sudden weight of the turtle, then 'Trim!' we shouted again as it flopped into the bottom of the dingy and their counterbalance was no longer required. Flippers, claws and beak thrashed and snapped as we secured and 'stuck' it, then all was quiet again as the blood poured out into the waiting containers.

We had found that we could sharpen the stainless-steel blade on the back of the broken raft knife if we persevered for long enough, so that the problem of finding a way in to kill the beast became a little less arduous. Robin and Douglas imbibed their usual portions of blood but Lyn and Sandy declined, preferring to draw the serum out of the coagulated blood to use as a gravy. Neil, like me, drank as much and ate as much as was offered of anything, good, bad or indifferent, as long as it wasn't salty.

Douglas expertly extracted the flipper bones while I rested from my labours, dissecting the main part of the meat. Neil extracted the fat and a small harvest of eggs and looked on interestedly as I cut out the heart, at Lyn's suggestion, before we dumped the remains overboard. Two hours later we gazed in satisfaction at the large pieces of turtle steak hanging from the stays and set about cleaning up the boat and ourselves. Our tattered clothing, mine in particular, was now very bloodstained, both with the turtle blood and my own, for I usually sustained cut fingers and clawed arms in the confined space of the dinghy.

We were all improving steadily in condition now, our sores and boils had started to heal and although the storm had taken heavy toll of our energy we generally felt much more rested than during our frantic bailing and blowing marathons in the raft. The cramped conditions in the dinghy gave rise to bitter reproach and argument when tender limbs were trodden on or kicked, but we were becoming used to the feel of the boat. We were all instantly conscious of a small angle of heel and moved to correct it.

Our noon position 7°23′ North, 225 miles west of Espinosa again aroused us to talk of the coastline of Central America and our likeliest landing place. Douglas and Robin discussed the problems of rowing in the hot sun and as we poured sea water on each other to ease our discomfort in the equatorial heat, that particular problem was brought home to us with considerable force, and I told them we would only be able to row at night unless the days were overcast.

As the afternoon sun moved round the northern horizon to the west, three boobies flew close, then one, of the red-footed species, landed on top of the oar which served as a mast; then the other two, after circling a little, also came in to land. They perched on the paddle which was used as a spar for the sail, one on each side of the first. We all looked at Neil but he shook his head and grinned, pointed to the turtle meat and said 'We hae meat and we can eat.' The boobies made a fine figurehead and we watched with delight as they preened their feathers and spread their beautiful wings and tails, then as they eyed the meat speculatively we decided that our hospitality didn't extend to a meal, they could get their own easily enough, so we politely tipped them off their perch.

The evening brought quiet seas and calm weather, a glorious sunset and a peacefulness of the spirit. We sang the old songs of Scotland which the children loved to hear, for they carried a story with them. We sang Welsh songs for Robin whose Welsh inheritance did not, alas, extend to the musical traditions of the Welsh people (he was tone deaf); Lyn sang Brahms's lullaby as a special nightcap for the twins, and as twilight deepened and watches were set, I felt that we had already gone beyond thinking in terms of survival. We had started living from the sea as an adapted way of life, for not only were we surviving, we were improving our physical condition. As we settled to rest, I pondered the philosophies of advocates of 'at sea' living. To my mind there was little prospect of man developing a cultural relationship with the sea, in the way that he has done with the land; the predatory emotions which are brought to the fore to make living possible in this primitive style are not compatible with emotional beauty or intellectual finesse. However, we no longer thought of rescue as one of the main objectives of our existence; we were no longer subject to the daily disappointment of a lonely vigil, to the idea that help might be at hand or was necessary. We no longer had that helpless feeling of dependence on others for our continued existence. We were alone, and stood alone, inhabitants of the savage sea.

### Twenty-sixth day

The calm of the evening before was short-lived, and as cloudy, squally weather came up from the south, *Ednamair* tugged at the half-tripped sea anchor and we moved to the north-east again. Rain showers followed the squalls and we huddled under our flimsy sheets for shelter, the bailer scraping its monotonous rhythm from time to time. Towards dawn, *Ednamair* yawed alarmingly and almost broached to, with the bursting wave-crests rearing high above the starboard side of the boat. The sail had collapsed as the dinghy's bow fell away from the wind and as it filled again, *Ednamair* straightened out to meet the

seas. Now thoroughly awake from my doze, I heard Lyn say
that she couldn't see the float (Douglas had constructed a monocle from a lens belonging to her broken spectacles, but it was
now giving trouble) so I lifted my head above the bow canopy
and searched the area of sea where the float should have been;
there was no sign of it; I reached forward under the bow canopy
and pulled at the sea anchor rope—it was slack. The sea anchor
and float had gone and I wondered, as I prepared to stream the
spare sea anchor, what sort of fish could have taken the other
one so quietly; there were quite a few I could think of, but the
cleanly severed anchor rope and the tripper line told me nothing.

Although we were making better speed than with float and
sea anchor streamed, the risk of 'broaching to' with our six-
inch freeboard was too great, and the spare sea anchor was
streamed, half-tripped with two ropes attached, one of them a
thick piece of polypropylene which would certainly give most
predators indigestion; it also had the advantage of floating on
the surface so that we could see it both by day and by its
phosphorescent trail at night.

Squally weather conditions continued throughout the day,
Douglas and I alternating at the helm to steer *Ednamair* through
the worst of the seas. Our noon position of 7°30′ North, 210
miles west of Cape Espinosa gave us encouragement to take
advantage of this favourable south-westerly wind, for if we were
suffering from the buffeting that the dinghy was receiving we
were also making good progress in the right direction; later we
started shipping water in increasing quantities as the waves
became higher, so we opened out the sea anchor and hove to
with reefed down sail to avoid being swamped by one of the
rogue waves which sometimes ran at right angles across the
crests of the wind-driven seas.

Towards evening Lyn had just finished her routine of tending
our various skin ailments and seeing that the twins performed
their muscle toning leg exercises, when a strangely uncomfortable feeling came over me; at first I thought I was going to be
ill, then looking hastily around and grabbing a piece of sail
cloth, I realised that for the first time in twenty-six days, I was
about to have a bowel movement! The experience was exhausting and left me weak and trembling for almost an hour
afterwards, but the satisfaction of knowing that my body was

again functioning normally was encouraging. An hour later
Douglas followed suit and though he was the last person to
display physical weakness, the effort left him weak and helpless
for some time afterward. This gave Lyn cause for concern that,
while the others, including herself, showed no real signs of
discomfort, there must come a time when our bodily functions
would revert to normal if our increased intake of solid food was
maintained. She therefore planned a second course of enemas
for herself and the twins the following day, Robin once again
declining the services offered. I was tempted to order Robin
to have one, for the dangers of an intestinal block were to be
avoided while water was still available for the enema, and before
any signs of ill-health from such a stoppage became evident,
but I also felt that to destroy his prudish reserve at this time
might also adversely affect his chances of survival, so I decided
that while he maintained all the outward appearances of good
health, we would leave him in peace and keep a close eye on
him. As Robin had the largest physical frame in our group, I
automatically gave him a larger ration than the others so that
his body condition should be closely similar to our own. I also
felt that, as the only person outside our family group, he could
be watching for some signs of discrimination against him, a
natural enough fear in his situation, so I tried to ensure that
this did not happen, and often incurred the wrath of my own
family by this apparent display of favouritism.

Robin's strong strain of human sympathy made up in many
ways for his practical inability, and his unshakable belief in
our eventual rescue, and our ability to survive until then, was
a spur to my determination to ensure that such a satisfactory
conclusion to our ordeal should be reached.

We talked into the night of various ways of cooking omelettes,
pancakes, chapatties and oatcakes, and put them in the tea-
time menu for Dougal's Kitchen, then lay back listening to the
rough seas surging around the dinghy's hull as she pitched in
uneasy restraint at the curb of the sea anchor.

### Twenty-seventh day

The rough southerly wind which had blown throughout the
night had kept us awake and anxious. We had steered *Ednamair*

from time to time in the breaking seas to help keep the bows pointed in the direction of the surfing combers and now, as dawn approached, the seas quietened in the dying wind and with half-tripped sea anchor we steered an east-north-easterly course into the sunrise.

Sandy and Neil slept heavily in the morning after a night of unease trying to find comfort in the pitching bow of the dinghy. Exhaustion had overtaken them about four o'clock and they had slept until eight and awakened with hunger as their next instinctive desire. After a breakfast of turtle meat and eggs, Lyn set about the morning routine of airing the pieces of sail which we used as bedding, a simple task in the quiet sunshine, but more difficult on days of flying spray. After spreading the remaining turtle meat to dry we brought out the tins of turtle fat, now swimming in beautiful golden oil. With a dipper apiece Lyn and I collected the valuable oil drop by drop, taking great care to avoid any sediment, until we filled a small perspex jar with the golden liquid. We then filled one of the empty water cans as well, collecting about two pints in all. We now had not only a medium which Lyn proposed to use for enema purposes, but also like the apothecary's panacea for all ills, a health-giving liquid that could be taken internally, rubbed on externally, used as a lubricant for tools, and it would even smooth the waves should the need arise.

Lyn administered a small water enema to the twins and herself that afternoon without result, all the fluid being retained, so she decided to try them with a turtle oil enema on the morrow. In the meantime she rubbed a little of the oil on our sore parts to make them partially impervious to the salt water and to minimise the risk of our developing pressure sores, for in our cramped conditions we had difficulty in keeping the weight off our buttocks and bony parts. My sunburned rear end was now healing at last and I was able to lie on my back again without breaking the skin on the burnt patches.

Our noon position of 7°33′ North, 190 miles west of Espinosa put us another twenty miles nearer land for the day's run.

I had decided to try the spear at last and that afternoon I sat on the centre thwart, spear poised, watching the dorado swoop to and fro under the boat. I had often passed an hour tensed up in this position awaiting the right fish at the right moment, an exercise in patience and endurance, for to hold the spear poised ready to thrust with all the power at one's command, at an instant's notice, is an exercise in reflex action which civilised men have long forgotten. At about three o'clock in the afternoon, one of the smaller dorado, about ten pounds, flashed under the boat and, turning on its side, tried to catch a small minnow which sheltered under a small piece of sheet trailing in the water. The white underbelly of the fish showed clearly only about two feet below the surface of the water and I thrust with all my strength, feeling the armed point strike the fish and penetrate. With a sudden jerk, I felt the spear tip break, then the fish was gone. Ruefully, I surveyed the product of my afternoon's work. It had broken at the barb again; I would have to find an alternative way to catch fish for there was no other wood that I could use. Discouraged by the failure of the spear, I thought that if only I had fastened a line to the spear tip, no, if only I had tipped the spear with a fish hook, that was it! I needed a gaff of sorts and I could make one too! It would mean that I'd have to strike up instead of down but I was sure it would work. I set to work immediately to cut grooves and notches in the right places on the spearhead and paddle, working steadily until dusk.

Late afternoon chatter centred around Dougal's Kitchen again. We would serve coddled egg and cheese pasties with butter, and minced beef pasties to a special recipe of such savoury goodness that our mouths watered in imaginary delight. Surely the public would flock in their hundreds to sample these beautiful delicacies; why, we wondered, had nobody thought of them before. We not only enjoyed the thought of ourselves consuming these beautiful pasties, but also of the hungry farmers on market day, thronging the homely precincts of the kitchen and wolfing large quantities of food, at a modest profit to ourselves, of course!

We settled down to the discomfort of another night with warm thoughts of savoury odours and satisfied customers, our own miserable bones making harsh contact with the fibreglass hull, resting awhile in one position until 'pins and needles' warned us of restricted circulation, or cramp locked our muscles and made movement imperative, and with movement the inevitable chain of disturbance to the others.

### Twenty-eighth day

The weather deteriorated during the night watches until by morning a rough southerly swell rolled up under us, tossing *Ednamair* in a twenty foot cycle of uneasy movement, the small cross swell making for much discomfort as the crests slopped aboard with each roll of her bows, making it necessary for us to bail frequently. The sluggish lift gave me cause for concern and calling Douglas to take over the helm, I exchanged places with the twins in the bow and detached the bow canopy so that I could examine the flotation collar. As I leaned over to look, a wave washed right over it into the dinghy. 'Give me the knife,' I called, stretching my hand behind me, watching a large green-crested comber bearing down on us. I hesitated, thinking of replacing the canopy to try to shed as much water as possible, but the knife was thrust into my hand at that moment and with a quick slash I cut the ropes which held the flotation collar to the bow. The collar dropped heavily into the water as the bow rose high in the air, the breaking sea creaming past beneath us. Quickly I cut the other lashings and then poked my finger into the non-return valve at one end. Water spurted out from the sleeve and a cursory examination showed the holes worn around one end where the rope lashing had chafed the collar. *Ednamair* had been trying to keep afloat with a millstone round her neck! I detached the collar completely and lifted one end into the boat, slowly draining the water out of the other end until the ten-foot sleeve lay crumpled and empty at my feet, then taking a length of fishing line, folded the leaking end up and lashed it firmly with the heavy nylon until it was airtight again. Fully inflated once more, it was secured to the plunging bows with strong tape instead of rope to try to avoid a repetition of the chafing, and the dinghy rode easily again as the float controlled her pitch and protected her bows from the breaking seas. With the canopy refastened we snugged down again, very little water being shipped inboard, and the bailers rested from their labours.

Our noon position at 7°40' North, 180 miles west of Espinosa gave a good day's run of nearly fifteen miles with the sea anchor streamed fully open, and as wind and sea eased in the afternoon it became unnecessary to steer; the sail was made fast again and with the sea anchor half-tripped we resumed our progress to the north-east.

Robin played host to our selection of Desert Island Discs that afternoon, and a fine talent he had for the job too. Our choices of recordings surprised each other, and sometimes ourselves, for we now placed different values on them than those of mere entertainment or nostalgia. The youngsters chose much more serious music than we had expected, and while I tried to sing as many of the classical pieces selected as I could remember it was the difficulty of remembering some at all that surprised me. Pieces like Elgar's Enigma Variations for Robin, music to the ballet Coppelia for Douglas, Bizet's Symphony in C for Lyn, Beethoven's Violin Concerto for myself, I could not recall a a single note and yet they had been as familiar to me as my right hand. Of others like 'Finlandia' for Robin, Lalo's 'Symphonie Espagnole' for Lyn, Beethoven's Ninth and Moussorgsky's 'Night on a Bare Mountain' for Douglas, I had almost total recall. Recordings of Scottish songs were favourites with Douglas and the twins, Welsh ones for Robin; songs by Mary Hopkins were chosen by Robin and Douglas, and Lyn's choice of Wagner's 'Siegfried Idyll' was also mine, for we had often listened to it together when our love was new and extravagant. My attempt to sing it nearly ended in tears but I managed to swallow the lump in my throat for the first few stanzas. Neil chose 'South of the Border' and Sandy the theme song of 'Dr Zhivago'. 'Cool clear water' for Lyn was highly popular, and her 'I'll take you home again, Kathleen' was, like my 23rd Psalm, chosen for childhood memories. Vocal recordings were most popular, but not all songs. Lyn wanted readings from Dylan Thomas, whose

> Do not go gentle into that good night . . .
> Rage, rage against the dying of the light

she often quoted to encourage us in times of stress. Douglas requested Gerard Hoffnung's after dinner story 'The Bricklayer' and I wanted a good Scots voice to read Robert Burns to me. Selections of books ranged from some obscure works on statistics for Robin, the Oxford Book of Verse for Douglas, Chekhov's plays for Lyn, and a comprehensive study of marine,

plant and animal life for Neil, Sandy and me, so that we would
know what we were eating.

We had had our fill of culture by tea time and turned to the
tantalising thought of rowing for the coast when we ran into
calmer weather. We had no rowlocks for the oars, so I would
have to make thole pins to use in their place. There was no wood
strong enough, but a U-shaped steel tube from the bellows was
about the right size so we brought it out from under the stern
seat; I handed it to Douglas. 'Exercise your muscles on that,'
I said, 'I want it broken at the bottom of the U.' Slowly the
bar straightened then bent again as Douglas flexed his biceps,

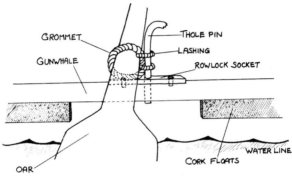

Projected rowing fixture

then it broke at least an inch too far on one side of the U.
'Sorry,' he said, grinning all over his face. We tried the pins in
the rowlock sockets. They fitted quite nicely, and with a
grommet lashed to them to take the oars we would be all set,
apart from water. We couldn't row without fresh water in much
larger quantities than we had been used to, and that meant a
large container—we didn't have one. We did! The flotation
collar! If it was going to be calm enough to row, it would be
calm enough to do without the collar and we could fill that
with enough fresh water to sink the dinghy! (This was no
exaggeration for our freeboard was so small that if only six
inches of water accumulated in the bottom of the dinghy it
would add enough weight to make swamping almost unavoid-
able in anything but the smoothest of seas.)

We went to rest with hope in our hearts and no rage at all against the dying of the translucent hues in the tropic sunset, for the wind was dying with it and we had the promise of a gentle night.

### Twenty-ninth day

We made good headway in the gentle westerly breeze throughout the night, with the sea anchor tripped and *Ednamair* making over a knot to the east-north-east. The rising sun guided our daylight progress and the business of survival resumed its daily routine. I had barely started work on my gaff when, looking down into the sea past the flashing blue, green and gold of the dorado, I spotted the brown shape of a shark, but it was the first small one I had seen since my short-lived love affair with the one on the raft. This one was catchable too. We had caught a flying fish in the night, a very small one, so I put it on the large hook and weighting the line heavily I cast well out to clear the scavenger fish. My baited hook drifted down past the shark and at first I thought he was going to ignore it but after it came to rest he turned and nosed towards it. Douglas, stretched across the dinghy in my usual place beside the thwart, called: 'What're you doing Dad?' 'Catching a shark,' I said calmly, watching the shark nose a little closer. 'You're bloody mad,' Douglas said, sitting up quickly; Robin, too, was sitting up apprehensively and Lyn said 'You mustn't.' 'Good old Dad,' said Neil and Sandy from the bows. 'I'm having him,' I said watching tensely now, as the shark reached the bait; the moment I felt him touch I would have to strike, for if he got the nylon line between his teeth he would bite through it like butter. I was going to try to get the steel shank of the hook between his jaws. He was over it now, I felt the contact with tingling fingers and struck swiftly, the line exploded into action, he was hooked!

He fought with alternate periods of listless acquiescence and galvanic action, twisting and plunging savagely to rid himself of the hook. I was afraid of the line breaking but I feared more the arrival of a larger shark which would attack the hooked one. Slowly, foot by foot, he came to the surface, the line cutting deep into the heel of my hand. Lyn sat ready in the stern, paddle in hand. The shark broke surface, struggled savagely and plunged deeply. I had to let him go, he was still too strong, but he was a nice five-footer. A Mako shark, Douglas said (he was our shark expert) and I'd hooked him in the eye! Back up he came. 'We'll have him this time,' I grunted, my hands aching. 'Be ready to take the line, Robin . . . I'm going to grab his tail and pull him in that way.' Excitement rose high in the dinghy; Robin and Lyn looked a bit uncomfortable at being given the biting end to look after, but were determined to do their best. (I knew he would break free if I tried to haul him in head first by the line.)

The shark surfaced again; gingerly Robin took the line from my hand as I quickly leaned over and grabbed the shark's tail. 'Trim!' I shouted and Douglas leaned out on the other side of the dinghy. The harsh skin gave me a good grip, and with a quick pull the shark lay over the gunwhale. 'Lift its head in now!' I kept a firm grip on the tail as Robin lifted the struggling fish inboard with the line. Lyn rammed the paddle into the gaping jaws and they clamped shut on it. Knife in hand I leaned forward and stabbed it through the other eye; the shark struggled then lay still. Giving Douglas the tail to hold, I stabbed the knife into the slits of the gills behind the head, sawing away at the tough skin until finally the head was severed. 'Right, you can let go now!' I felt like Bruce after Bannockburn. We had turned the tables on our most feared enemy; sharks would not eat Robertsons, Robertsons would eat sharks! Quickly I gutted out the liver and heart: a solid thirty-five to forty pounds of fish with very little waste apart from the head. We breakfasted on the liver and heart, then Robin chewed the head, watching carefully for the razor-sharp teeth while I cut strips of white flesh from the almost boneless carcase. It was tougher than the dorado but juicier and we chewed the moist strips of shark meat with great relish.

Our larder now began to look good; long strips of shark swung from the forestay while the remains of the turtle meat had dried nicely. I cut out the jaw bone from the shark's head while Lyn and the twins cleaned the spinal column. We had lost all our Indian necklaces from the San Blas Islands, the most valued of which were the shark's teeth and backbone necklaces. Now we had the raw materials to hand and time to spare to make our own!

Our noon position of 7°50′ North and 160 miles west of Espinosa showed our better progress and though the weather had become overcast and unsuitable for drying the shark meat, at least it afforded us a little shade from the hot sun.

I set to work on the gaff again and Douglas steered while Lyn and Robin tended the hanging fish and meat. Robin had become rather edgy these last two days and now, under Lyn's exacting instructions, he became petulant and stupid, leaving jobs unfinished and making little attempt to put things right when the fault was brought to his notice. I had to speak sharply to him and to check his work to make sure it was done as he had been told.

During the afternoon we had noticed that the water which had been decanted from one of the tins was foul so that we now checked and found that, of the remaining cans, four of which were unopened, one more was unpalatable, being full of black sediment, and one was brackish where salt water had trickled in from the waves washing in on the stern seat. There was still a gallon and a half of water in a plastic bag, so that we were not unduly worried, but I decided to test it to make sure it was fresh. It was good water and we settled down to our various chores again. Lyn had found a foot of stout copper wire in her sewing basket and I was getting the germ of an idea about constructing a more efficient gaff than the model I was working on.

Lyn had given the twins a small turtle oil enema in the early afternoon to try to ease their blocked systems and now Sandy was responding. Our nickname for the bailer, which we still used for urinating to save trimming the boat when its use was necessary, up to now had been 'pissoir', for there had been no need for a receptacle of any other sort in our constipated condition, but now, after a short conference in the bow, Neil shouted, 'Pass the shittoir, Sandy wants to go!' Sandy's experience was not nearly so exhausting as Douglas's or mine, and Lyn thought that the turtle oil had helped in this respect.

As we watched the pieces of shark swinging against the clearing sky in the evening we felt some satisfaction that with the turtle meat already in store we had enough food to last us for a week, plus some of the emergency rations which were reserved for the children's 'little supper' before they went to rest.

### *Thirtieth day*

The gentle breeze fell calm during the night and at dawn the promise of another dry day was reflected in the sunrise. The limpid blue of the sea flashed as the dorado sped under and around *Ednamair*, then the cry of 'Turtle!' from Sandy made us move hastily to our positions clearing the dinghy for action.

A large stag turtle nosed curiously at a trailing rope, and with a swift grab we secured first one then both back flippers. A wild struggle ensued, for this was a tough one and with painful lacerations to our hands, we finally landed him, lashing out wildly with clawed flippers in the bottom of the dinghy. We secured him, Douglas holding one flipper and snapping beak, Neil and Robin a back flipper each, and myself a front flipper under my knee to have both hands free for the coup de grâce. The tough hide made difficult work of it and we all sustained bruises and cuts to our legs before the deed was done and the turtle lay quiet. It was well past noon by the time the meat was hanging and the shells and offal dumped. It had been tough work, but the meat was a good deep red and tastier than usual. Neil had helped to collect the fat and Douglas had done his stuff on the flipper bones. Robin had finally been persuaded to help Neil collect the fat but he didn't seem to have much liking for the job. We nursed our wounds and cut the meat into small pieces for drying in the hot sunshine. The shark was still occupying the rigging, so since there was no wind, the sail was taken down and the small pieces of meat spread out across the stern seat and the centre thwart while we all crouched in the bottom of the dinghy, limbs overlapping in the cramped space.

We lunched well on shark and fresh turtle meat, nibbling at turtle fat afterwards and crunching the bones to extract the rich marrow from the centre. We were all blessed with fairly strong teeth and although the rest of our anatomy suffered in many degrees from the privations we had undergone, our teeth remained clean and unfurred without any external assistance from brushes. The diet obviously suited them!

The sun shone all day, but we suffered it gladly for the drying meat and fish needed every minute of it. The quicker it dried the better it cured so we poured cups of salt water over each other to keep cool and turned the meat over at regular intervals.

It was only when I was making up the log for the day and was about to enter up the small change in our position since noon the day before, that Neil leaned across to me and whispered, 'Hey, Dad, put this in your log. On the thirtieth day Neil had a shit.' I looked to see if he was serious; he grinned an impish smile and said 'It's right,' so I put it in. It was, after all, a fairly remarkable incident and that's what logs are for, as well as the routine remarks.

While our skin problems were generally improving in a slow sort of way, my hands had become a mass of hacks and cuts. Every time we caught a turtle I usually collected one or two cuts to mark the occasion and this, aggravated with sticking fish-hooks into myself, brought the combination of cuts and old boil scars to a pitch where I looked like the victim of some ancient Indian torture. Yet after the initial hurt of these cuts they gave me very little pain and I wondered if the salt water anaesthetised them in some way.

Evening threw quiet shadows over the sea as we packed the drying food under cover for the night. The small pieces of turtle were placed in one section of Lyn's bamboo sewing basket, while the shark strips, now smelling pretty strongly, were

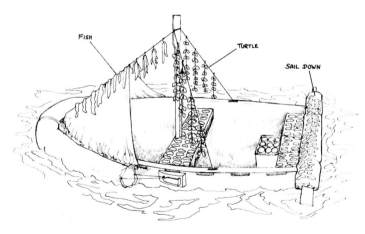

A good drying day

placed in a separate piece of sail. The sea was almost mirror calm and loud splashes broke the unaccustomed silence as dorado leapt after flying fish. A louder splash made the sea foam, as a larger predator, probably a shark, attacked a dorado which leapt desperately to escape. The fins of the larger sharks were never far away but we ignored them now as long as they left us alone.

Dougal's Kitchen came into the conversation as we chewed our shark strips. Robin described the various catering systems and the range of menus he had encountered, but we decided to stick to a minimum of uncomplicated dishes: pasties served in cold weather (sheep's head broths and hambone stock lentil soups) and a special sort of Scotch egg and cold chicken pasties with a proper salad in summer. However, in order to accommodate our expanding appetites, we opened a small private room catering for special dinner parties and here we really let ourselves go with curries, shish kebab, stroganoff, exotic Chinese foods and luscious salads.

The evening planet Jupiter reflected a sinking path in the calm sea while Antares in the constellation of the Scorpion gleamed a warm red in the zenith above us. I was watching the Southern Cross just slanted past the meridian to the south when Douglas called excitedly to me from the thwart: 'I can see it Dad, look!' I twisted my head round quickly, but saw nothing remarkable in the direction of his pointing finger. 'It's the Pole star!' he said. We were unlikely to see the Pole star under 5° North latitude so this at least roughly verified our latitude; we were back amongst friends!

### Thirty-first day

*Ednamair* lay quiet under the brilliance of the night sky. Phosphorescent trails streaked the sparkling surface of the sea as marine life darted in profusion around us. Deeper down, large patches of glowing green fire moved swiftly in pursuit of a smaller quarry, while more scattered areas of luminescence glowed brightly and faded again in response to some unidentified stimulus. It seemed the whole world of marine life lay below us, locked in spectacular but deadly combat in the struggle to survive. Dorado patrolled the vicinity of our little craft with brilliant moonlight reflecting from their silver scales as occasionally they lay quiescent on their sides showing their pale underbellies. A sudden splash followed by a heavier bump under the keel indicated the presence of a heavier fish and Robin, on watch, grabbed a paddle and poked at it. I leaned over the side in time to see a huge shark glide under the boat, bumping us in passing. I grabbed the broken spear, and thrust at it on its return, striking the shark on the back, and though it gave no sign of alarm when the blunt point made contact, it didn't return. It was the biggest specimen we had seen to date, larger than the dinghy, but it made no attempt to attack us.

Dawn found us in our usual state of torpor, finally sleeping after a night of restless movement to ease our sore limbs. I sorted the drying strips of turtle and shark, and after they had been rehung, surveyed them with some satisfaction. We were starting to build a reserve of food again which would be useful if our initial landfall was inhospitable or if for any reason we ran out of turtles. I eased my cramped, twisted posture and turned to watch Robin pour the water from the plastic bag into the drinking jar preparatory to breakfast. Lyn asked him to check that the bag was properly fastened, for it was slung too near the mouth of the bag to be safe, and this was followed by Robin's usual petulant protest and eventual 'Oh! I'm sorry!' and his agreement to see to it.

The cry of 'Turtle!' (this time from Neil as he felt it bump under the bow) had us all fully alert and we hurriedly cleared the stern area as another stag turtle investigated our fibreglass, bumping its shell against the keel. We were now expert turtle catchers and our team work was a smooth sequence of move-ment as the turtle was swung aboard, flapping wildly like the previous one. The fresh meat from this turtle would allow us to preserve the meat from the last one which would be added to our reserves, so I set to work with a will to perform the execution and the subsequent carving of the joints of meat. We needed a reserve of meat if we were to start rowing, for working oarsmen get hungry as well as thirsty and at the end of it all, we had to be fit to cope with the emergencies that were bound to arise if we made a landing on the beach. To die through weakness at such a point would make our present struggle a futile gesture against fate.

Lyn assisted in stripping out the shell blubber and expertly removed the fat covering the intestinal wall, for hanging and subsequent oil extraction. We enjoyed a luncheon of fresh turtle steak and meat juice with the now coveted marrow bones for chewing afterwards. The marrow's taste differed with each turtle, and the bitter-sweet taste of this one provoked a wide variety of comment. We speculated on the possibility of residues of strontium 90 in the marrow, transferred by marine life from the French atomic testing grounds in the Ocean current sequence to this area, but living with continuous danger had blunted our fear of more remote threats to our welfare and we gnawed with vigour, grateful that our teeth were our own and able to withstand the onslaught of primitive usage. It was not until the shell was finally disposed of that we found the empty plastic water bag, knocked from its lashing by the struggling turtle, lying in the bottom of the dinghy. We turned, unjustly, on Robin with bitter acrimony and rebuked him for his carelessness. There had been reason enough to regard Robin's practical skill with suspicion and with an important thing like water, there was little excuse for my neglect to see that the water bag had been safely stowed. I had grown careless in the relief from anxiety about the food reserves and was now reaping the harvest. I lifted the bag, blood dripping from its crumpled emptiness, and handed it to Robin. 'Better wash it out in salt water,' I said. 'See that it's rinsed before you fill it in the next rain.'

Our noon position of 7°55′ North and 145 miles west of Espinosa only illustrated how little ground we had covered in the last two days and with the added worry of a water crisis thrust upon us, our mood of complacency in the morning had changed to one of impending disaster in the afternoon. The loss of the water bag was serious for it left us with only eight pints in the tins and two of these were foul. I could see no signs of rain and set to work immediately to finish work on the gaff. If we were to run out of water, only turtle or dorado could save us. Turtle came only when it suited them but the dorado were there for the catching and it was on these I had to concentrate.

The hot sun beat down on us in the afternoon, drying that part of the fresh meat we had hung in the rigging and curing the already half-dried meat spread on the thwarts. We stoically endured the blistering heat, seeking shade from pieces of sail and coolness by evaporation, rinsing our clothing with sea water. Evening clouds were of the alto-cumulus type, affording no prospect of rain, and as we packed away the dried shark, savoury smelling like smoky bacon, we felt rather depressed at this sudden threat to our existence in the form we dreaded the most. We had had a good day in the food stakes, but food was no use without water.

The dorado were moving close to the surface in the calm sea and I decided to try my gaff immediately. I had fastened the hook with the heavy nylon fishing line and it was very secure with two lengths of the hundred-pound breaking strain line fastened from the eye to the grooves cut into the shaft paddle handle, the lines being bound tightly to the spear shaft to make the whole weapon as rigid as possible. I had also fastened a reserve line from the hook directly into the boat and this was fastened to the mast. The business end of the gaff was lowered over the side and I waited for a suitable fish to come within striking distance. They were not in the least alarmed by the presence of the weapon and swooped around *Ednamair* in their usual fashion. I was tensed ready to strike and an air of expectancy hung over us, for we had cleared away the box of water cans in anticipation of landing a fish. Slowly I turned my hook in the direction of a small female when, with almost no warning, a medium-sized bull dorado shot over the gaff. My reaction was almost instinctive and I struck upwards into the fish. The sudden weight of the fish on the hook made my heart leap. 'Look out!' I shouted as I pulled upwards to bring the fish into the boat. There was a sudden heavy pull on the handle and the fish was gone, the hook with it. The reserve line was also broken. I looked at it foolishly for a moment, then cursed myself for an idiot. The reserve line should not have been fastened at all, it should have been held by one of the others ready to play out in the event of the first two breaking, for if the two broke, how could I expect the other one to hold until the fish had been played? I pulled the gaff in and looked at the end. The lines had parted close to the hook where they had been bound to the shank of the spearhead; the fault lay in the whole thing being too rigid for the materials I had available. I looked round the boat at the disappointed faces of the others and thought I also detected an attitude of scepticism at my thinking to secure even one of these powerful fish with the crazy equipment I had fashioned.

In the gathering twilight I settled down with the knife and stripped off all the broken nylon line and secured fresh line in its place. I had one hook left and if that was lost, then we would have to depend on turtles entirely (which, apart from the lucky shark strike, was what we were doing now!). Darkness closed in with the new gaff unfinished and we settled down quietly for the night, silent with disappointment.

Lyn took Douglas's watch that night as well as her own, and in the night hours I talked with her of the farming life we had left behind us in Britain. The old frustrations and anxieties of our life together at that time welled up between us and I told her I would never go back to that despairing life of nagging and bitterness engendered by the poisons of poverty and hardship. I had told her there was more to living than the brutish exist- ence which resulted from the change to modern farming methods, where animals were business machines, living or dying by virtue of their profit margins, the animals themselves be- coming as devoid of character as the cages, stalls or cubicles in which they lived, known only by a number, until death put a merciful end to their existence.

The simple process of talking of them brought the bitter memories of our personal life before us, and of the way depriva- tions and long hours of toil, day after day, had eroded the happiness from our lives. The barrier of bitterness which had gone from between us with the nearness of death rose once again to divide us, and Lyn wept as I flung savage recriminations at her for the years of nagging and misery, before I lapsed into the silence of arid repentance, finally asking and receiving forgive- ness. The declining moon illuminated our brief reconciliation before we lay down to rest, reserving the saliva in our already dry mouths.

### Thirty-second day

After a night of breathless calm, and brilliant starlit beauty in the sombre hours after moonset, morning brought a hot sun in a blue cloudless sky. I had finished work on my second gaff and it was ready for use, a triple nylon line leading from the eye of

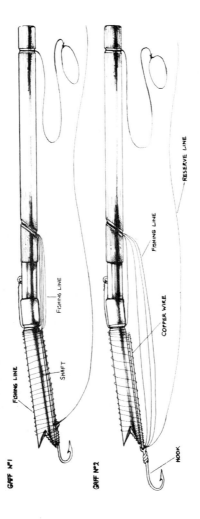

Improvised gaffs

the hook's shank direct to the grooves in the handle so that on striking the hook would have freedom to swivel within the limits of the arc of the short line. I felt sure that this time it would work unless the line itself was faulty. We were down to six pints of water now and still no prospect of rain so that some alternative source of water was imperative if turtles were not available.

We had finished breakfast and I was about to clear the stern of the dinghy prior to another attempt with the gaff when thankfully, I heard the cry of 'Turtle!' from Douglas. He pointed to the scaly head surveying us from fifty feet away and we hurried to clear the space. 'Another one!' shouted Sandy pointing to the starboard bow where a stag turtle had appeared near the anchor rope. I was toying with the idea of killing them both when the stag turtle suddenly spotted the other, a female. There was no hesitation; like a flash the stag joined with the female, mated, and then both disappeared beneath the surface. Desperately we scanned the surface for signs of their return but they were gone. I had always assumed that the turtles had sought our company because they thought we were a little island, but now I felt pretty sure that we were sought out as a prospective mate; I made a mental note that we were unlikely to capture any females with eggs while there were any stags around, and turned back to my gaff. The boys were looking very disappointed and now as I lifted down my improvised fish catcher they resigned themselves to some more of my fooling about. Lyn was particularly cross, both at our losing the turtle and at being upset by another fishing episode and nagged with bitter reproach, starting a long and fruitless harangue about the conditions to which she had been subjected throughout our married life. How I had failed to provide the normal civilised amenities on the farm, how the roof had leaked, the stove hadn't worked properly, of the years without electricity or telephone, the lack of money and the neglect of the children's education and social life. The whole gamut of bitterness and frustration as the wife of an overworked and underpaid small farmer rose up within her and I snapped and snarled back with equal savagery until she burst into tears and Sandy cried 'Stop!' Robin comforted her quietly with his 'Oh! Come on now—' but I was unrepentant and looking crossly at her I said 'Lyn, if you don't be quiet and stop nagging, I'll leave you and go to sea!'

I gave the reserve line to Douglas to hold and told him to make sure that if the fish broke loose from the gaff, with the hook, he was to give it plenty of slack and play it slowly. Tensely I watched the dorado swoop under *Ednamair*, my muscles aching, as they hunched to act on a split second reflex. 'Shut up!' I snarled at Lyn talking to the twins. 'How the hell do you expect me to concentrate with you gossiping away!' Several large fish cruised around but they were over the forty-pound mark, too big; a smaller dorado slanted under the keel. I lowered the gaff a foot, I could feel the silence; a larger bull swooped towards the smaller one and it turned away, right across my striking path. The swift upward hook, the surge of weight, a gleaming arc of silver and pandemonium as we fell on the wildly struggling fish in the bottom of the boat. I grabbed its tail and cut it off with two swift strokes, then groping forward, severed its head; it was ours! We looked at the twenty-pound fish with glee. 'Thank you, my love!' I looked in astonishment at Lyn, now all smiles, and said: 'Do you mean to tell me that this bit of fish can change you from a—' 'Yes,' she interrupted smiling sweetly, 'Come on, what are we waiting for?' We ate some of the flesh for lunch but concentrated mainly on the juicy liver and heart, and after I had cut the flesh away from the backbone, we severed the vertebrae and sucked the spinal fluid from the cavities. Robin, chewing at the head (his favourite piece for browsing over), found that the large eyes were nearly all moisture, and by sucking reduced them from an inch in diameter to something the size of a small pea. The gaff had worked well but in the scramble after the fish the copper wire which held the hook rigid for striking had broken, so I abandoned fishing for the day.

We celebrated our arrival at latitude 8° North and 135 miles west of Espinosa by not having any water with our lunch, and prepared to spend a hot afternoon in cooling streams of sea water and watching the developing cumulus clouds for signs of precipitation. We had laid out the drying turtle to complete its cure and had hidden the pieces of fresh dorado away from the sun to retain as much of its moisture as possible. Our hopes of rain developed with the clouds, and when we saw a shower falling in a black curtain on the horizon, we opened another tin of water to ease our tortured mouths. Four showers passed us without even coming near, and as the light westerly breeze ruffled the surface of the placid ocean, the clouds diminished in size and drifted away to the north-east.

We sucked the moisture from the raw fish until there was nothing left in our mouths but fibre, and talked of dishes we would serve in Dougal's Kitchen on a hot summer day. Cold consommé, a special recipe of Scotch eggs and salad, fresh fruit salad and ice cream (we dwelt on that one a while!) and long, long drinks of cool fruit juices. At tea time, toast and tomato sandwiches, pancakes écossais, and lamingtons (a chocolate and coconut covered jam filled sponge) would be served.

With five pints of water left between six of us, we had much need to use our imaginations. I quietly told Lyn and Douglas that we would only have sips of water from now on and the moisture we could obtain from fish. The spectre of thirst had already settled on Douglas's face, his eyes deeply shadowed in his skull sockets. Robin seemed to be in better shape physically than he had been after his seasickness in the beginning; he now paid more attention to the details of any work he was given but the thought of a wasted gallon of water preyed on his mind. Lyn was untiring in her ministrations to the twins, tending their eyes, their skin ailments, massaging their legs with turtle oil and exercising their limbs. She bathed us when we were hot and rubbed us when we were cold, saw that the sheets were clean and dry and nagged and badgered us into a form of cleanliness where every move was an effort. I decided to overhaul the gaff in the cool of the morning and tried to rest; my mouth was dry and foul tasting, my tongue searched my gums for saliva, and found none. With eyes shut and lips pressed firmly together I thought of a long cool draught of milk. I felt the salival moisture return and the desire for water ease a little. It was going to be a hard night, for sleep would not come to ease the burden of thirst. The boys' distress increased sharply with their inability to lose their misery in hours of oblivion. They tossed and turned restlessly, complaining at each other for usurping an extra inch of space or fold of sheet. Robin's muttered delirium was interrupted only by the sipper jar (the only mediator which won mutual approval) and it circled only twice in the night.

### Thirty-third day

I set to work at daybreak, the calm sea showing barely a ripple as the windless dawn flushed pink in the clear sky; no clouds, no rain. I overhauled the gaff carefully, testing the tension of the lines and adjusting the angle of the hook, now closer to the end of the spear shaft on the shortened copper wire. We cleared the space in the bottom of the dinghy to give room to work and took down the sail so that I could have a clear swing inboard.

Slowly I lowered the gaff into the crystal-clear water, my nerves taut and muscles trembling with expectation. Dorado swooped close under the stern, six of them, and turning in graceful unison, swam slowly along the side of the dinghy. I struck wildly, missed completely then relaxed as they scattered; that was not the way to catch fish! Lyn handed me a sip of water and wetting my mouth, I allowed my nerves to quieten. A single female cruised six feet down. I angled the hook towards its path and suddenly there were two more close by gliding up from the bow across the line of strike. The gaff swung, I felt the hook bite then detach and hold again as the lines took the strain. 'Look out!' My shout was unnecessary as the fish, twenty pounds of bone and muscle, performed a graceful arc into the bottom of the dinghy and thrashed wildly at our feet.

There are two places to catch and hold a dorado. One is where the tail joins the body, as already described, and the other is at the eyes. Placing the thumb and middle finger in the eye sockets and pressing firmly seems to have a paralytic effect on the fish. To try to hold these very strong, very slippery and wildly struggling fish in any other way usually ends up with the fisherman helping the dorado over the side into the sea again. Their whole existence depends on their ability to leap after flying fish and the simple two-foot hurdle formed by the side of the boat is no obstacle to them in regaining their freedom. Therefore the moment of relaxation comes only after the fish is dead, for many have been lost after a successful landing. Knife in hand, I held the gaff clear to try to avoid it being damaged amid the struggling bodies as Douglas, Robin and Sandy grappled with the fish. Finally as Douglas held its eye sockets, I dropped the gaff and caught the tail, knuckles bruising on the fibreglass as the fish lashed its imprisoned frame. A few seconds later, we surveyed the long blue and gold body as it turned to silver, even in death a thing of great beauty. I disliked killing these fish even more than the turtles, but likes and dislikes do not enter into the survival stakes; eat or be eaten is the law of survival at sea, our choice was clear!

'We'll have two more,' I said, panting with exertion. 'We can do with the water they contain.' My blood-spattered hands readjusted the hook on the striking end of the gaff. The ideal place to plant the hook was in the area under the body the first six inches behind the head. The fish was then compelled to swim towards the pull of the gaff whereas, if the hook was inserted too near the tail, the powerful thrust of the tail took the fish away from the pull of the gaff with a considerable increase in dynamic tension, resulting in the breaking of the lines. The second one came aboard five seconds later, a smaller one this time and hooked much too near the tail, but it almost ran into the gaff as I lowered it. Fortunately it was only a fifteen pounder.

We all rested a little after the demise of this unexpected offering from the sea and looked at the two shining fish lying in the blood-spattered water in the bottom of the dinghy. 'Clear them forward a bit,' I said. 'We don't want to be slipping on them with this next one.' It was with great care that I lowered the gaff for the third strike; five minutes grew to ten, to fifteen, my shoulder muscles ached with tension and the boys fidgeted in their places, but I was wiser now that we had two in the bag. I wasn't going to risk our last hook on a chance strike, it would have to be the right place in the right fish. A beautiful bull dorado surged under the keel, about twenty pounds. Swiftly I struck at it, touched it, but failed to plant the hook, then to my surprise a female, attracted by the flash of the bull's sudden evading tactics, swam straight towards me. I struck up, felt the hook give as it went home, then anxiously I felt something snap. I shouted a warning to Douglas, holding the reserve line, then risking all or nothing heaved it into the boat. The hook parted from the fish as it landed in the bottom of the boat and Sandy grabbed its tail as I fastened my fingers in its eyes, its mouth snapping at the heel of my hand with needle sharp teeth. It was a twenty-five pounder and we surveyed our catch with satisfaction as its struggles died away, the colours still changing in the iridescent skin. (Dorado change colour rapidly when under stress and will alter from blue to green to gold or silver in quick succession.)

We could certainly get enough water from these fish to avoid the necessity of opening another tin of water until the evening and provide some enjoyable eating as well. On examination the gaff was found to have one broken line, one of three from the paddle handle. When the strain had come on the hook the tension was unevenly distributed but the two remaining lines were fortunately strong enough to take the strain.

As we gutted the fish, Lyn investigated the stomachs and found two flying fish, recently swallowed, inside. We added these to the livers, roes and hearts, sucked the eyes and the spinal fluid, then cut some of the flesh into strips for drying and saved enough wet fish for meals for the day.

We had established a certain amount of security at least with forty pounds of fish drying and a good quantity of turtle meat already dry; we needed only water now, but it looked as if we were going to have to depend on fish for our drink. The sun rose in a cloudless sky as the day advanced and the sea, mirror calm, reflected the glare of the sun under our pieces of sail so that by noon we wilted in the furnace of the sun's rays. Listless and weary, I poured salt water on Douglas and Robin then passed the bailer to Lyn who similarly soaked the twins. We clutched pieces of sail and canopy over us to escape the direct rays of the sun and sweltered in the over-hot shade we created. We poured water on the sails to stop the heat conducting through and radiating to our bodies. Some small fleecy cumulus appeared but gave no sign of developing to clouds of rain-bearing capacity. The fish dried on its own, unheeded and untended.

I simply allowed a ten mile easterly drift for the day's run, we were going nowhere of our own volition and this was neither rowing nor sailing weather. The flaming orb of the sun crept slowly down to the western horizon, a horizon that was now a clean-cut straight line in the calm seas instead of having its usual lumpy appearance, for there was hardly a sign left of the trade wind swell. We followed the sun's progress inch by inch, our drought-stricken mouths silently counting the minutes till the sun would set and allow us our next sip of water (not because it was sunset but because that was when we could start moving around without unnecessary exhaustion). Carefully I opened a tin of water and decanted it into the jar then, taking the mug, I measured out a small mouthful each. Eyes gazed fixedly at the jar as the mug was passed round; I made sure each had an equal share and drank it; the time for rationing had arrived. A small piece of wet fish each constituted our supper, our talk stilled by the need to conserve the moisture in our mouths.

Douglas's deep-set eyes searched the horizon, not for ships, but for the high-reaching cumulus of a rain cloud; the skin of his cheek bones was drawn taut, sharply etched against the white sail. Robin stirred in his sleep, muttering to himself, then sat bolt upright talking aloud in semi-delirium. I measured another sip of water each (the twins had a little extra to go with their private ration of fortified biscuit) and mouths moistened, *Ednamair's* crew settled quietly to rest again. An hour later, Douglas excitedly called me to look at a ship's lights on the horizon. I asked him to look carefully again before I disturbed the sleeping twins and the disappointment crept into his voice as he saw the light fade and disappear. There are many explanations for these lights, the most common on a clear night being that of a setting star, refracted to several times its normal size, appearing momentarily through a gap in the cloud layer, just before setting or after rising, on the horizon. Thirty seconds' scrutiny usually serves to discount this illusion; Lyn and Robin both called me on their watches to verify the same illusion with different stars. The beauty of the starlit night was not lost on us even in our arid physical condition and we gazed in rapt silence at the breathtaking grandeur of the stars glowing in the depths of the Milky Way. We were very small fry indeed in these oceans of space. I could hear Lyn's voice quietly praying as I dozed, but then as I looked into the limitless heavens I could only think of FitzGerald's verse from the Rubaiyaat of Omar Khayyam:

> And that inverted bowl they call the sky,
> Whereunder crawling coop'd we live and die,
> Lift not your hands to it for help, for it
> Rolls impotently on as you or I

not because I thought the verse was apt but because I liked the rhythm of the words and the assessment of our importance to the universe. The night crept slowly on through the muttered delirium of Robin's dreams, the twins restlessly turning in a fruitless quest for ease which only water could bring.

### *Thirty-fourth day*

As daylight approached, we all lay sleepless and unrested. We scanned the small cumulus coming up from the south for rain clouds; it seemed the upper atmosphere had wind even if it was calm at sea level. The water jar was empty and we eyed the remaining four tins with longing. As soon as there was enough light, I repaired the broken line on the gaff and we cleared the decks for fishing. Robin, Sandy, Douglas and I sat in the stern section; Lyn talked quietly with Neil in the bows. My mouth, dry and foul tasting, bothered me and distracted my attention from the fish as I tried, unsuccessfully, to work up a saliva. My eye caught Lyn's, she motioned with her hand in a gesture of drinking and pointed to Neil. I couldn't see him but the thin shank of his leg told me what Lyn was trying to say. 'Let's have sippers before we start,' I said. 'I can't concentrate.' Robin opened the can with alacrity and Douglas poured it into the water jar. I measured out our ration, each a half inch in the bottom of the mug, then passed the jar to Lyn. 'Hold on to that,' I said. 'We don't want it broken.'

I turned once more to the fish and found myself gazing at a twenty-five pound female dorado about to go under the boat while two enormous bull dorado lazily eyed the *Ednamair* as they glided past. They looked between sixty and eighty pounds apiece. I waited for the smaller fish to return and angled the hook in readiness; it came with a rush, flashing from under the keel at high speed; I jerked the gaff towards it in a belated reflex action, then as I watched it turned sharply in a right angle after the bulls. My hook struck with a satisfying solidity and then detached from the end of the gaff with a heavy jerk. I pulled sharply and as the fish flew in a graceful arc into the dinghy, the hook came out of the fish and fell away. 'Grab it!' I yelled as it thrashed amongst legs and arms. Sandy, on his knees, groped after the slippery body, Robin stuck his legs out like a soccer player trying to keep his hands off the ball and the fish, with a great leap, used his knee as a stepping stone and vanished with a splash over the other side of the boat. I cursed them all generally and Robin in particular. 'Why in hell's name can't you keep your bloody knees out of the way?' I snarled (the fact that there wasn't any place else for him to put them seemed immaterial). 'In future, use your hands and,' I added maliciously, 'it doesn't matter if the bloody fish bites you, it'll have hold of you, even if you haven't got hold of it!' Robin gazed at me unhappily with mute reproach and tucked his knees awkwardly into the side of the dinghy.

I lowered the gaff again after readjusting the hook and waited for my nerves to quieten. Slowly I relaxed and watched the fish approach, gleaming blues and green, gold and silver, but none in the right place for a strike. Twenty minutes later I still waited, nerves stretched to the limit as I angled the hook towards the flash of the fish, trying to assess the size and direction of the beast before I struck; a fifteen-pound female suddenly came down from the bow, I struck at it, missed, but the fish turned attracted by the flash of the hook. My second strike was accurate, an inch behind the head and under the belly; a second later our breakfast was aboard. Douglas dropped the line and had it by the tail almost as it came over the gunwhale and the knife finished its struggles in a matter of seconds. It wasn't a big fish but it would have to do. I cut up the flesh and handed out pieces of spine to suck. The twins had an eye apiece and we all chewed the liver and roes.

That white-hot disc of fire we call the sun beat mercilessly on our little craft that morning. Lyn and I bickered at each other until Lyn dissolved in tears; Robin, the psychological conciliator, with good intent, made the grievous error of coming between husband and wife of twenty years' standing and was promptly used as the butt of our wrath. (He was pretty resilient, was Robin!) Douglas shouted 'Turtle!' and our quarrels were forgotten in the flurry of clearing the necessary space and getting the trim right. The turtle bumped the side of the boat and Douglas reached down and grabbed it. As I waited for Robin and Douglas to swing it aboard, the lengthening silence made me anxious. 'Come on, let's have it!' I said. 'It's gone, I let go of it!' Douglas's voice was contrite with misery. 'You what?' I yelled. 'Why the hell don't you leave it to me if you can't manage!' Furious, I slapped his knee with my open palm. 'That's right, hit him, you big bully!', Lyn's voice from the bow. We stared at each other in silence then slowly I lifted the box of empty water cans down off the thwart and lashed it in position. We spent the rest of the morning contemplating our own misery, without even the benefit of companionship to ease our thirst.

Noon however brought gathering cumulus in the southern sky and our position of 8°05′ North and 120 miles west of Espinosa (93°20′W) restored a little sweetness to our bitter thoughts, for I announced that we should now be about 380 miles from the coast, two-thirds of the way there, and if rain came we would be able to make it in eighteen days by rowing at night. The early afternoon found us chewing pieces of wet fish to moisten the dryness of our mouths and leathery tongues. Another can of water was opened to wash our mouths clean of any salt residues from the fish (it was kept in sailcloth moistened with salt water) and as we watched the rain showers develop, we stared at the falling curtains of rain, many miles distant, with hypnotic intensity as if willing them to come towards us. It had already been our experience to have a shower spend itself before reaching us, while heading in our direction, so we resisted the impulse to indulge in drinks all round when a large curtain of rain crept towards us. By four o'clock, we knew it must hit us and as the sky darkened, the relief brought saliva unbidden to our mouths. We passed the jar round in an un-rationed sip and then as large isolated drops fell around us we turned our faces to the sky, mouths open to catch the first drops while the salt was washed from the sail and the canopy.

We had decided to use the sail to collect water instead of the rubber sheet, to see if we could collect a supply of water that didn't taste of rubber. The sail was not exactly impervious to water but it held it long enough to allow it to be collected. The raindrops grew in size and intensity, the main curtain of rain now almost upon us, and we eagerly sipped at the puddles gathering in the sail to test for salinity. The sail was clear first and as the main weight of rain started to cross us, the welcome sound of water pouring into tins was music to our ears. I reached for the second can and Robin was filling the jar, when, as suddenly as it had started, the heavy downpour fell to a sparse patter of drops; we gazed blankly at the retreating curtain of rain, churning the water only a few hundred yards distant, but moving faster away from us than we could ever hope to chase it. Desperately we scooped the remaining drops into the cans, nearly three pints gathered but one of these, from the rubber bow canopy, was brackish and unpalatable. It was half an hour before we silently folded the sail into the stern and slumped back in our places. After a quiet word with Lyn, I passed the brackish tin of water and she administered it by enema to the twins. Four pints altogether and a little in the drinking jar. I gazed resentfully at the now distant curtain of rain then shrugged, it was better than two! I brought out the gaff and sat watching the fish swoop under the dinghy. 'Come on,' I said to Robin and Douglas recumbent in the bottom of the dinghy. 'Clear away and stand by for a fish, if we can't get water one way it'll have to be the other.'

Thirty minutes later I was still waiting for a fish to swim within striking distance. The large bull dorado glided temptingly close but the smaller ones kept a respectful distance. 'Change me places,' I grunted to Robin; we carefully eased across to keep the trim. Two minutes later I struck at a twenty pounder and felt the sense of relief flood into the marrow of my bones as the fish thrashed wildly on the floor of the dinghy. Sandy, his face contorted with pain, gripped desperately at its tail while my fingers sought and found the eye sockets. I cut my thumb in my haste to finish it off and was nursing my wound when I noticed Sandy was weeping and holding his knuckles. He had held on like a limpet despite the beating his skinned knuckles had received between the fish and the side of the dinghy. I put my arm round him and comforted him, wondering how it was that Sandy, at twelve, had so much practical common sense.

As we sucked our drops of spinal fluid and ate the pieces of wet raw fish in silence, the clear evening sky held no prospect of rain. Lyn prayed again. It seemed to lift her burden of worry and anguish for the twins and helped her to feel less alone. 'Our Father, which art in Heaven, hallowed be Thy name.' Her voice was quiet as we listened to her repeat the Lord's Prayer after putting the twins to rest. Robin suddenly choked on a piece of bone and Lyn quickly gave him some biscuit and fish flesh. It seemed to do the trick and we settled down to wait the night out.

### *Thirty-fifth day*

We watched with unbelief as the darkness of cloud grew in the southern sky, the great piling cumulus rising to the archway of heaven itself to blot out the stars. We felt the pores of our mouths tingle with the stress of anticipation as the saliva failed to generate in our too dry gums. I passed the jar round. 'Sippers only, till we know for sure.' The dawn brought rain. An hour of nice, heavy, beautiful rain. We filled the containers, tins and plastic bag (Robin's privilege) then filled our shrunken stomachs to uncomfortable distention. Lyn gave Douglas, the twins and myself another enema, and to our surprise we all, including Robin, had bowel movements shortly afterwards, holding on to each other as we perched on the gunwhale to perform.

Robin felt redeemed now that the plastic bag was full again, and we were able to take water from it by means of a spout which I had fastened in one corner, without untying the neck, so that the risk of a repetition of the cause of the previous loss was much reduced. We ate dried turtle meat again, now that water was available, and the taste of the savoury strips of turtle steak was most welcome after our enforced diet of wet fish. We also tried some of the dried shark, which had a much stronger taste than the dried dorado, and there was no doubt that the tangy tongue-biting flavour was distinctively pleasant so long as there was plenty of water to go with it.

The cry of 'Turtle!', just at noon, had us scrambling to clear the stern area of the box full of water cans as the head of a curious female turtle appeared a few yards from the starboard bow. We licked our lips in anticipation of eggs for lunch, then as I remembered Douglas's difficulty with the last one, I called out that nobody was to touch it until I could get to it. Robin, who was nearest, called out that it was well within his reach and that he could get it easily. 'Robin!' we all said together. 'Change me places, Robin,' I said. 'It's better to be sure.' Lyn joined in urging him to leave it alone, but with a new-found confidence he reached over and grabbed a flipper. Seconds later the turtle was gone from his ineffectual grasp, and once a turtle has been

held it seldom returns a second time. I could hardly believe it
had been so stupidly lost and anger surged through me in a wave.
I turned on Robin, striking him with my open palm, hating his
stupidity with savage intensity. 'You stupid bastard!' I shouted
at him. 'Why the hell don't you do as you're told!' Robin
rubbed his face with his hand. 'It's a good job this isn't a rugger
field. It'd be a different story,' he said threateningly. Anger
swept me again. 'If this had been a rugger field I'd have broken
your bloody jaw!' I snarled. My hand reached for the paddle
handle. 'If you disobey an order again I'll hit you with this!'
I was beside myself with rage. He looked at me with his contrite expression and muttered something about dropped
catches at cricket. I felt helpless at this confrontation with
stupidity. How could I persuade this boy that not only his, but
the lives of my wife and children depended on our ability to
hunt and catch food? He knew and acknowledged that Douglas
was much stronger than he, and that Douglas had been unable
to hold the last one. He had been told to leave it and had
deliberately disobeyed, and when confronted with his irres-
ponsibility, sought refuge in the cricket field. This survival game
was not cricket; if you dropped a catch you starved! I turned
away in disgust. 'Put the things back again,' and the water cans
and bric-a-brac from under the stern seat were stowed back in
position. I looked at Robin, opened my mouth to deliver a
lecture then shut it again. At twenty-two, I could hardly expect
to reform him in his unpractical ways, but I made a mental
reservation to thump him with the paddle first if he reached for
another turtle.

Our noon position of 8°10′ North, 115 miles west of Espinosa
showed little progress and with rain once more in the offing my
thoughts turned to rowing again. We needed more food reserves,
particularly turtle, and a bigger water storage capacity. My
eye went to the flotation collar, and as a matter of routine, I
leaned over to check the fastenings; the tiny spurt of water from
under the rope prompted me to investigate further; it was half
full of water again from a hole chafed in the other end from the
one I had previously repaired. After the collar had been inspected, we established the presence of not one hole but five,
two in the middle and three in the valve end. After untying and
emptying the tube I lay back to rest and try to think my way

out of this one. I could not see any possibility of repairing the holes, but with no flotation collar, we were living on the razor's edge, with no support for us or the dinghy if we were swamped in rough weather. I looked at the holes again and sat awhile, racking my brains to find the answer. There was none, except the possibility of trapping some air in the sleeve by bending the tube over and lashing it in the middle as well as the end, and I didn't have any suitable line left except the fishing line. I suddenly had a better idea. 'Hand me the knife,' I called to Douglas. With quick strokes I cut the tube in half where the two holes had been. I now had two pieces five feet long. I fastened the piece with the good end to the centre thwart, open end up, and lashed it in position. This ,' I said, 'is our reserve water tank; it'll hold about seven gallons and as soon as we have it washed and half filled, we'll start rowing!' I looked at the other piece. If we were swamped, it was big enough to support the weaker swimmers while Douglas and I got the dinghy afloat again, and the fishing line would not be needed anyway until we reached the coast. I felt delighted with this compromise and by evening, had almost forgiven Robin his stupid behaviour of the morning. I suddenly felt alarmed; if Robin rowed he'd be sure to drop the oar over the side; couldn't miss! There would have to be a foolproof fastening on these.

As the twilight deepened into night, the faint breeze from the south ruffled the surface of the sea and I warned the watchkeepers to be on the alert for squalls later on. With no flotation collar, rough weather could mean the end for us. Only Douglas and I shared the full import of this knowledge; I felt it would be an unnecessary burden to the others to labour the point.

### Thirty-sixth day

Slowly the wind rose from the south. At first it was a fine gentle breeze, then blew with increasing force until the breaking tips of the waves gleamed in the darkness.

As *Ednamair* pitched and yawed, shipping more and more water over the midships section, I set Douglas steering her into the waves while I opened the sea anchor out and adjusted the trim of the dinghy to keep a high, weather side. The squalls strengthened and Douglas and I stood watch on watch, helping the tiny boat through the violence of the rising seas. Lyn and Robin were still unable to steer so that they took over the bailing when necessary. I felt uncomfortable without the assurance of the flotation collar and prepared a strangle cord on the water sleeve to enable me to make it into an airtight float very swiftly if an emergency arose.

The squalls brought rain, intermittent and of moderate precipitation, to make the night cold and uncomfortable. We bailed and sang songs to keep warm, the memory of drought too recent for us to feel churlish with the weather. Collecting rain water became difficult in the strong wind but we managed to gather enough to rinse the salt out of the sleeve and put a half gallon of good fresh water into it before the rain finally tailed off into a drizzle. The wind eased with the rain, and dawn found us shivering and huddled together, eating dried turtle and shark to comfort our sodden skins. The turtle of yesterday was forgotten in the discomfort of the new day.

Each day had now acquired a built-in objective in that we had to try to gain as much as possible over our reserves of stores and water until there would be enough in stock to get us to the coast. I looked upon each turtle as the last, each fish as the one before I lost the hook, by an error in strike. It only needed a six-inch mistake to make the difference between a dynamic pull of about eighty pounds and one of a hundred and eighty with the consequent breaking of the unevenly tensioned lines, and I knew that sooner or later it had to happen.

Lyn washed and mended our clothes, which now had the appearance of some aboriginal garb. Douglas had only his shirt left (Lyn was trying to sew his shredded undershorts together in some attempt to make him presentable when we reached land); Lyn's housecoat, now in ribbons, was more ornament than use, and my tattered underpants and vest were stiff with turtle blood and fat. Robin and the twins were in rather better garb, for their labours made less demands on their clothing. I suppose we would have been thought a most indecent lot in civilised society. (On second thoughts, I've seen some weird products of modern society whose appearance was rather similar so that perhaps we would merely have been thought a little avant-garde.) Robin and I had beards with unkempt

moustaches which hung over our upper lips; salt water boils
and scars covered our arms, legs and buttocks and were scattered
on other parts of our anatomy, intermingled with clawmarks
from turtles, as well as cuts and scratches from other sources.
The adults were not desperately thin but the twins, Neil in
particular, had become very emaciated. Knee cramps troubled
us from time to time, but generally speaking, apart from Sandy
who had a slight bronchial cough which Lyn's expert ear had
detected the day previously (for she had a constant fear of a
static pneumonia developing in our cramped situation), we
were in better physical condition than when we had abandoned
the raft. Many of our sores had healed and our bodies were functioning again. We were eating and drinking more, and our
ability to gnaw bones and suck nutrition from them increased
with our knowledge of the easiest ways to attack them. We were
no longer just surviving, but were improving in our physical
condition. As I looked around at our little company, only Neil
gave me cause for worry for his thin physique made it difficult
to determine whether he was improving or not, and though he
was a most imaginative child, he seldom complained unless in
real physical pain. Lyn was careful to see that his supplementary
diet was kept as high as possible, and I scraped bone marrow
to add to the twins' turtle 'soup' (a mixture of pieces of dried
turtle, meat juice, water, eggs when available, and fresh or
dried fish).

Our thirty-sixth day ended much as it had started; wet, cold
and windy, seas slopping into *Ednamair* as she bounced in the
steep short waves, the bailer's familiar scrape and splash, and
the helmsman hunched on the stern and peering at each wave
to determine its potential danger to our craft. Robin, trying to
snatch forty winks in his 'off' time, suddenly sat up with a cry
of distress. 'There's no meat on my bone!' he shouted. Then
looking at his thumb (which he had been sucking) with a
puzzled expression on his face, he lay down to sleep again. The
twins chortled in the bows for an hour afterwards. Late that
evening Sandy said he thought he must have 'done it' accidentally for there was diarrhoea all over his clothes. I passed Sandy
over to Lyn while I cleaned up the sheets moving Neil around
to get the muck cleaned off the dinghy when Lyn said 'You'd
better send Neil along when I've finished with this one, Sandy

hasn't done anything at all!' Neil's voice full of injured inno-
cence came from the bow, 'Well, how was I to know?' We
chortled for half an hour over that one!

### Thirty-seventh day

Our gratitude at the arrival of dawn lent warmth to our bodies
and as the heavy shower slackened to a few scattered drops, we
stopped bailing, the sea calmed by the heavy beat of the rain.
Douglas and I had steered through the night, Lyn and Robin
bailing whenever the breaking waves had broached our defences.
Daylight made the helmsman's task a lot easier for he could
then see well in advance the high or the rogue wave which might
upset us. Breakfast of dried turtle, dried fish and plenty of drinking water heartened us, and Lyn set indefatigably about her
morning chores, handing the sheets to grumbling Robin to
hold for drying. Douglas honed away at the turtle knife bringing
it to a better edge (one couldn't exactly call it sharp any more)
and the twins laid out the dry stores under the canopy to give
them an airing, for a light mould quickly gathered on the
surface of the dried food in this damp atmosphere.

As the sky cleared we brought out the fish strips and fastened
them to the forestay, refastened the plastic bag containing the
turtle fat, now swimming in golden oil, and drained the oil
from the boxes of fat, one of which Robin had upset when he
carelessly thrust the paddle handle under the stern seat; it took
him over an hour to clean the slippery oil from the bottom of
the boat. Douglas, taking pity on Robin's uneducated fingers,
patiently instructed him in the art of tying hitches and knots
until our activities came to an abrupt halt with the cry of
'Turtle'. I eyed Robin and Douglas grimly. 'This one's mine,
touch it before I tell you if you dare!' We cleared the stern of
the dinghy quickly as the turtle bumped alongside, another
stag but a good-sized one. I leaned over and caught hold of the
shell, then the back flipper. He fought strongly. 'Right, grab a
flipper!' I called to Douglas, sitting opposite me. He caught the
other back flipper, then as the turtle threshed around, let it go
again; I had loosened my grip on the shell and was now gripping
the flipper with one hand and the sudden increased weight
nearly caused me to lose my grip. As the turtle tried to dive

under the boat my arm was fully extended; the hand on the
end of it didn't feel as if it belonged to me at all as the edge of
the shell cut into my wrist. With a heave I had the turtle back
to the surface and Douglas once again secured the other back
flipper. We transferred our grip as the struggles eased and in a
trice we had the turtle turned around and hoisted aboard.

As it lay on its back in the bottom of the dinghy, beak
snapping and flippers going like windmills, I gasped for breath
from the exertion and wondered if we were just growing weaker
or if this was a particularly strong turtle. Perhaps a bit of each,
I thought as I watched Robin try to grasp a flipper with both
hands, and fail. I caught up the knife, 'Let's get on with it,'
and started the three-hour struggle, pausing frequently for a
rest as each stage of the killing and dressing of the reptile
proceeded. After the initial coup de grâce it sometimes took as
long as half an hour before the next stage could proceed after
the bleeding; we still drank the blood, even though there was
now plenty of drinking water, in order to derive all possible
nutrition available. Finally when the job was done and the
dripping meat hung from the stays prior to being cut up into
small pieces for drying, we stopped for a meal of dried dorado
and fresh steak soaked in the delicious meat juice which did
much to restore our flagging spirits. The estimated day's run
which put us at 8°15′ North and only 95 miles west of Espinosa
(over one knot with the sea anchor full open) gave us further
cause for satisfaction.

The chart indicated that we were now approaching the direct
route between Panama and Hawaii and so the possibility of
sighting a ship was greater than of late. The indifference with
which this little snippet of information was received was a
source of satisfaction to me for now that our hopes were pinned
on making a landfall, there would be no distress if a distant ship
ignored us.

We had no bailing to do in the afternoon, for the seas had
diminished, and the sea anchor was again half-tripped to allow
us to make better progress. The discomfort from the lumps of
meat swinging from the rigging and my insistence that the
thwarts should also be used as drying space for the turtle meat
made us cramped and irritable; already tired from the rough
night, Douglas and Robin started bickering over the position

of the box between them (an inch either way was a matter for grave dispute), and then Robin and the twins over the territory under the centre thwart. Lyn and I, in harmony for a change, decided that if they could still find the energy to argue, they must be getting better.

After a meal of fresh turtle meat and water we chewed a bone apiece and talked of Dougal's Kitchen. Percolated coffee, good quality English cheeses (Oh, how our mouths watered for the sharp taste of a Cheshire cheese!) and how the proper use of paper could take some of the drudgery out of restaurant work. The use of manufactured flavours came in for a lot of criticism in that it was being used to enhance the flavour of material which bore very little resemblance to food, and that subtle differences in flavour were fast becoming a part of restaurant history. The cry of 'Turtle' quickly brought us back to the Doldrums and we gazed at the very small specimen which was investigating the sea anchor rope. It wasn't much bigger than a soup plate and we decided to let it grow. As it came alongside Robin tipped it up by its shell and in a flash it turned around and bit savagely at his hand, drawing blood. 'Aaagh!' yelled Robin as we all admonished him, telling him to leave the little thing alone. Some time later, as the sun was setting, a larger female turtle came close and the temptation to have eggs for breakfast was too great. We would have to dress it in the dark but there was a moon later, and besides I could now do the job blindfold. Five minutes later I was drawing the blood from its neck arteries and as darkness fell I sawed around the shell and quickly sought the egg clutches on either side of the intestines. There were none! My disappointment was intense and I searched again, believing my knowledge of the turtle's anatomy to be at fault. Douglas checked to make sure; no eggs. Feeling much aggrieved, I set to work in the dark, feeling my way around with knife and fingers, cutting the meat away from the shell and severing the various knuckle joints at the expense of only one cut when the knife bluntly slipped off a shell joint and pierced the ball of my thumb (I hadn't got a mark there so far!). I finished in the record time of two hours.

We spent the rest of the evening talking quietly of the distance we could row in a night, and how long it would take us to reach the coast. I estimated that at three hundred and fifty miles it was about fifteen days away, and that if the weather allowed us to dry our present stocks of turtle meat we should have nearly enough dry material in hand. (Once the mast was taken down, it would be more difficult to dry the meat, and another support would have to be found for the canopy.) We still had well over three gallons of water in store too, and the night sky looked heavy with rain cloud. A good rain would allow us to fill the sleeve tonight! A vague excitement stirred within me as I decided that, if rain did come, we would fit the thole pins and make the grommets in the morning, ready to start the third and last phase of our voyage to land. I settled my head uncomfortably against the centre thwart and drowsed a little, moving my cramped limbs to ease the pressure on my buttocks (the twins' legs lay across the top of my midriff). Finally I gave up the attempt to sleep and stuck my head out beside the end of the canopy, looking at the gaps in the clouds, trying to assess what the night sky held for us. The back of my head found comfort against the gunwhale and I drowsed in a sitting position, my eye catching the glow of the moonrise as I looked around the horizon from time to time. A terrific blow on the back of my head nearly stunned me. My head burst with pain and I saw many stars that were no part of the firmament. Lyn's cry of 'Shark!' only dimly penetrated my singing eardrums. I turned my head in time to see the huge shape rush at the dinghy, flipping its tail to the surface as it scraped under the keel. It was that tail which had given me such a blow on the previous run and I grabbed the paddle to show the beast we had fight. Savagely I thrust the brass socket at its head and felt it jerk solidly as it made contact. The shark, longer than *Ednamair*, dived deep and left me to try to make the flattened brass socket round again.

### Thirty-eighth day

Daylight dispelled the vestiges of our disappointment over the turtle eggs, and after breakfast of some raw steak and the flesh of a scavenger fish (which I speared on the end of the knife) marinated in the meat juice collected overnight, we felt more able to see through the day. It hadn't rained much, and I had a good-sized lump on my head where the shark had left its mark.

A small shower, followed by some drizzle, had increased our
water reserves by a pint and the overcast sky gave little prospect
of a good drying day, but we hung out the meat in small strips
to make the most of it. A large white-tipped shark cruised near
by, reminding me of my lump, and the escort of eight pilot fish
in perfect formation across its back lent it the appearance of
an underwater aeroplane.

I prepared the gaff while Lyn and Robin sorted out the turtle
meat for drying and the twins readjusted the canopy and handed
out some strips of dried dorado which needed airing for an hour.
We now checked over our considerable amount of dry stores
every morning to ensure that it kept in good condition. The
fish strips quickly went damp and soggy in the humid atmosphere and the small pieces of turtle meat, if they were allowed
to become compacted, warmed up as if affected by spontaneous
combustion.

The dorado were reluctant to come near the *Ednamair* with
the shark still cruising around, but after we had made one or
two swipes at it with the paddle, it went away. I planned to land
another two dorado that morning, one for eating immediately,
to save the turtle steak for drying, and the other to increase our
already good stocks of dried fish. I angled the gaff towards two
likely bull dorado of rather a large size, then a large female shot
close above the hook; I struck swiftly and missed, but at that
instant a small bull of about fifteen pounds followed the female's
track and my hook sank into it in a perfect strike! The fish flew
into the dinghy with unerring precision and it was secured and
killed in the space of seconds. Feeling very pleased with ourselves, we admired the high forehead of the bull while I made
some adjustments to the nylon lines which weren't taking the
strain evenly, then I told Douglas to gut it and keep the offal.
I had noticed that although the dorado didn't eat the offal,
they gathered round curiously as the scavenger fish fought over
it. I had the idea a good fish could be taken unawares at this
time, so I had Robin throw some offal over just ahead of the
gaff. The scavenger fish rushed in, a boil of foam as they fought
over the scraps, while the dorado swooped close by. I chose a
twenty-five pound female dorado and struck.

The hook gave, then with a ripping sound the lines snapped
one after the other, and the gaff went light. I looked swiftly at

Douglas but he was pulling in the reserve line slowly. 'Didn't feel a thing,' he said. My initial reaction was one of extreme dejection; that fish had gone with our last big hook, no more fresh dorado. The nylon must have been cracked and I failed to notice; the tensions of the lines had been different too or they would have broken together; the disturbed water had probably distorted my aim, but it was no use being wise now, there wasn't another hook to be wise with. My spirits picked up a little as I realised that our stocks of dorado exceeded those of turtle meat and we had enough of both now to get us to the coast, even if we caught no more fresh turtle to supplement our rations. I still had another small hook to use for inshore fishing if that should be necessary, and if we felt like a taste of fresh fish I could always try a stab at another scavenger fish; we had been fattening them up for a while now, with our regular dumpings of turtle and fish offal.

Noon position 8°21′ North and 85 miles west of Espinosa, twelve miles nearer land, was not a great boost to our morale but I pointed out that throughout all the time we had been adrift we had either been becalmed or the wind had been favourable. There hadn't been a day yet when I had had to record an adverse run. The calming seas also indicated that we might soon be able to row although the heavy cross swell would have to diminish a little too before that would be possible.

Lyn bathed the twins that afternoon and after their daily exercises and a half-hour apiece on the centre thwart to move around a bit, they retreated under the canopy again as a heavy shower threatened. The dorado, caught in the morning, now hung in wet strips from the forestay while the drying turtle meat festooned the stays and cross lines which had been rigged to carry the extra load of meat from two turtles. We worked a little on the thole pins binding canvas on them to save wear on the rope, then realising that we were neglecting the most important job of making a flotation piece, took the unused piece of sleeve and started to bind one end with fishing line. The clouds grew thicker as the afternoon advanced; it was going to be a wet night again and perhaps we would be able to fill the water sleeve. Seven gallons of water seemed like wealth beyond measure in our altered sense of values.

I chopped up some dried turtle meat for tea, and Lyn put it

with a little wet fish to soak in meat juice. She spread the dry sheets for the twins under the canopy, then prepared their little supper as we started to talk of Dougal's Kitchen and if it should have a wine licence. As we pondered the delights of Gaelic coffee, my eye, looking past the sail, caught sight of something that wasn't sea. I stopped talking and stared; the others all looked at me. 'A ship,' I said. 'There's a ship and it's coming towards us!' I could hardly believe it but it seemed solid enough. 'Keep still now!' In the sudden surge of excitement, everyone wanted to see. 'Trim her! We mustn't capsize now!' All sank back to their places.

I felt my voice tremble as I told them that I was going to stand on the thwart and hold a flare above the sail. They trimmed the dinghy as I stood on the thwart. 'Right, hand me a flare, and remember what happened with the last ship we saw!' They suddenly fell silent in memory of that terrible despondency when our signals had been unnoticed. 'Oh God!' prayed Lyn, 'please let them see us.' I could see the ship quite clearly now, a Japanese tunny fisher. Her gray and white paint stood out clearly against the dark cross swell. 'Like a great white bird,' Lyn said to the twins, and she would pass within about a mile of us at her nearest approach. I relayed the information as they listened excitedly, the tension of not knowing, of imminent rescue, building like a tangible, touchable, unbearable unreality around me. My eye caught the outlines of two large sharks, a hundred yards to starboard. 'Watch the trim,' I warned. 'We have two man-eating sharks waiting if we capsize!' Then, 'I'm going to light the flare now, have the torch ready in case it doesn't work.'

I ripped the caps off, pulled out the striker and struck the primer. The flare smoked then sparked into life, the red glare illuminating *Ednamair* and the sea around us in the twilight. I could feel my index finger roasting under the heat of the flare and waved it to and fro to escape the searing heat radiating outwards in the calm air, then unable to bear the heat any longer, I dropped my arm, nearly scorching Lyn's face, and threw the flare high in the air. It curved in a brilliant arc and dropped into the sea. 'Hand me another, I think she's altered course!' My voice was hoarse with pain and excitement and I

Safety. The sea on the right has been calmed with turtle oil

felt sick with apprehension that it might only be the ship cork-screwing in the swell, for she had made no signal that she had seen us. The second flare didn't work. I cursed it in frustrated anguish as the priming substance chipped off instead of lighting. 'The torch!' I shouted, but it wasn't needed, she had seen us, and was coming towards us.

I flopped down on the thwart. 'Our ordeal is over,' I said quietly. Lyn and the twins were crying with happiness; Douglas, with tears of joy in his eyes, hugged his mother. Robin laughed and cried at the same time, slapped me on the back and shouted 'Wonderful! We've done it. Oh! Wonderful!' I put my arms about Lyn feeling the tears stinging my own eyes: 'We'll get these boys to land after all.' As we shared our happiness and watched the fishing boat close with us, death could have taken me quite easily just then, for I knew that I would never experience another such pinnacle of contentment.

# Part Three

# Safety

The high flared bows of *Tokamaru I* towered over us as she closed in, pitching and rolling in the uneasy swell. We emptied turtle oil on the sea to try to smooth it as the dinghy rocked violently in the cross chop of waves deflected from the steel wall of the ship's side; then, as they drew near enough, the Japanese seamen lining the bulwarks threw heaving lines, snaking through the air to land in the water beside us. The rise and fall of the dinghy was too great to make the line fast so I held it as we were pulled alongside the bulwark door. Willing hands reached down and we were hauled bodily through the bulwark door, Neil first, then Sandy. 'Come on Douglas, you next,' I said, as Douglas hesitated, waiting for his mother to go first, but to do so would have resulted in too much weight on one side and the sharks were still waiting. *Ednamair* bumped heavily as the swell flung her against the side of the ship; with aching arms I wound the line round my wrist and 'Right Lyn, on you go,' Lyn's legs kicked as she was hoisted aboard, 'Come on Robin, lad.' I looked at the empty *Ednamair* with sudden desolation in my heart, we must have her too! I threw the polythene bag containing the dried turtle and my log book, and one or two of the little trinkets from the sewing basket, on to the deck of the fishing vessel, then passed the line round the mast and brought the end with me as I was lifted to the deck.

Lyn, Douglas, Robin and the twins lay in a line along the deck and I wondered what was wrong with them, until I tried to walk and my legs wouldn't work. I clutched at the bulwark for support, then, to my dismay, saw the Japanese sailor cast off the *Ednamair*—they were going to leave her. I gestured wildly, for no one spoke our language, that we must have the boat as well but they shook their heads and held their noses. (I couldn't smell the fish and turtle drying on the rigging but to them it must have been overpowering!) I leaned out trying to catch the rigging and something in my appeal must have

reached them, for at a word of command from the bridge, they
brought boat hooks and lifted *Ednamair*'s stern up to the deck.
I grasped at the handles to help them but they motioned me
away, then they cut all the lashings to the mast, canopy, oars
and sea anchor, tipped *Ednamair* upside down and emptied
everything into the sea; with a heave *Ednamair* was brought on
deck. The sucker fish which we had thrown over from the
turtles were still clinging to the fibreglass bottom and were
knocked off as the hosepipe and brushes got to work in the
capable hands of the Japanese seamen. We smiled and said
'Thank you'. They smiled back and nodded, unable to communicate their understanding.

My blistered finger smarted painfully from the burn of the
flare as I staggered to the companionway leading to the bridge.
Pulling myself up with my arms I greeted the Captain of the
*Tokamaru* at the top and thanked him warmly in sign language
for the efficiency of his crew in spotting us. We could only
gesture for I had no Japanese and he no English, but gestures
were adequate. I produced my log book and we went into the
chartroom to check positions and to give details of who we were
and where we had come from, for as far as I knew we had not
yet been reported missing!

My estimated latitude at 8°20' North was good, only five
miles wrong, but my estimated longitude, though a hundred
miles wrong, was better, for we were a hundred miles nearer
land than I had estimated and would have reached it five days
sooner than I had said! We were rescued in position 8°15' North,
90°55' West. My estimate of 8°20' North, 92°45' West, without
sextant, chart or compass, wasn't a bad guess after thirty-seven
days adrift in the cross currents and trade drifts which compli-
cate that particular part of the Pacific Ocean. We had travelled
over seven hundred and fifty miles by raft and dinghy and had
about two hundred and ninety to go. We would have reached
the American Coastal shipping lanes in ten more days and the
coast in fifteen. Laboriously, I drew in on the chart the position
of our sinking, and pointed out on the calendar the date we had
been sunk. I drew a small picture of *Lucette* and the killer whales,
then wrote a list of our names and nationality so that our worried
relatives would know we were safe. The Captain nodded his
understanding and shaking hands once more he wrinkled his

nose and pointing at my tattered underclothing said 'Showa! Showa!' I could well imagine the powerful odours emanating from my blood and grease soaked rags though I could smell nothing. (I remembered how, during my days in the Mercantile Marine, we had picked up some survivors in the Karimata Straits near Indonesia after they had been adrift for ten days, and they had smelled with a pretty powerful odour then.) The only part of our bodies that seemed to be in no need of cleaning was our teeth! They were unfurred and felt smooth and polished to the feel of our tongues.

I staggered back to the foredeck where the family and Robin were seated with their backs against the hatch coaming, in their hands tins of cool orange juice, and a look of blissful content on their faces. I picked up the tin that was left for me, smiled my thanks to the Japanese who grinned broadly back at me, then lifting my arm said 'Cheers'. I shall remember the taste of that beautiful liquid to the end of my days. I looked at the twins, the juice seemed to be reflected in their bright eyes and their smiling lips, and suddenly my legs gave way and I flopped on the deck, holding my can of juice from spilling. We all laughed at my awkwardness and I crawled beside Lyn, sat down with the can to my lips and sucked like a child at the breast; mother's milk must taste like this to a hungry child, and I thought how lucky I was; an hour ago I had been ready to accept death and here I was, being re-born!

The Japanese crew carried the twins to the large four-feet deep, hot sea water bath, Robin and Douglas tottering along behind on uncertain legs. There in the fresh water shower (we had to readjust our ideas to the notion that fresh water could be used for other things besides drinking!) they soaped and lathered and wallowed in luxury, scrubbing at the brown scurf which our skins had developed, but this took many days to disappear. Then Lyn and I luxuriated in the warmth of the deep tub. The ecstasy of not having to protect boil covered parts of our anatomies from solid contacts had to be experienced to be believed, and the simple joy of soap lathering in fresh water is surely one of the greatest luxuries of civilised mankind.

New clothes had been laid out for us from the ship's stores and the kind concern shown us by these smiling warm-hearted seamen was almost too much for our shattered emotions. How

solution for patches. tried varnish but no g..
Everyone fed up blowing. Another flying fish
12 D'n Maas this morning, spirit of foul water
roof (shower). All in good spirits. — Lyn still c..
got through her day's work. watching for no sh..
can be dispiriting but we know we will be
picked up sometime. Play 20 Questions + I Spy
Est. Pos. Lat 2°06'N  230 W.? C Esp. One t..
visited in sight — below kindly — lives in co..
with Sandy's snores. Rations for about 12 da..
water)

20 £ (5 days) Continued N'ly course
esp. Pos Lat 9°40'N  long 240'& es..

**ELLIOT EQUIPMENT LIMITED** C.S.
**(One of the P. B. Cow Group)**
**LLWYNYPIA, RHONDDA**
**SOUTH WALES**

Day started at 4 a.m. when 25 lb Dolp..
jumped into Ed'w Maas. Quickly ha..
in jumped in + cut its gizzard + ..
off — returned to dinghy at 6 a.m. and ..
him up — some food eating fresh, the rest
day also dressed flying fish which flew aft..
into raft at midnight. Lynch on watch.
All well but no rain, f.. catching. Ho..
front moved East and over us today giving
for the future hope to amp today. All fel..show
fish very nice. Sunny day + good day.
21st (six days) abated midnight and
quiet night. It started ..

# Living in the Raft

These notes are generally applicable to all sizes of Elliot liferaft; allowance must therefore be made for apparent discrepancies in detail due to some rafts having more equipment in them than others or being of a different design.

## IMMEDIATE ACTION

One of the two large notices inside the raft gives the necessary advice. The second shows you how to inflate the various compartments and how to adjust the sleeve entrances.

## SEASICKNESS

It is most important to try and prevent the body being dehydrated by seasickness. One of your first actions therefore is to open the Ancillary

Relics. *Above*: 1—Sundry pieces from sewing basket; 2—Robertson tartan; 3—Social Security Card; 4—Neil's embroidery; 5—embroidered letter; 6—rain cape. *Below*: 1—Heliograph; 2—polythene bag; 3—sun glasses; 4—weight for fishing line (from pressure cooker); 5—fish hook; 6—Lyn's monocle

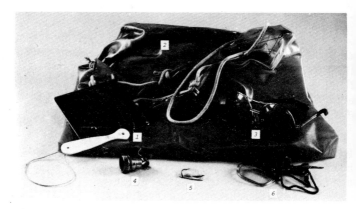

We still had some rations left: 1—'Little supper'; 2—'Crumbs';
3—fortified bread; 4—glucose sweets; 5—turtle meat

Rescuers and rescued: crews of *Tokamaru I* and *Ednamair* (left to
right—Douglas, Sandy, the author, Lyn, Neil, Robin)

cosy to have garments that were soft and dry. With the tingling
sensation of cleanliness came awareness of the rags we had taken
off, poor worn done things, they had kept the sun off and had
held the moisture next to our skins to keep us cool; they had
even, on occasion, helped to keep us warm when the night
winds blew on our rain-soaked bodies; now destined for the
broad reaches of the Pacific, I felt thankful that my bones were
not inside them.

On our return to the foredeck, there on the hatch stood a
huge tray of bread and butter and a strange brown sweet liquid
called coffee. Our eyes gleamed as our teeth bit into these
strange luxuries and in a very short space of time the tray was
empty, the coffee pot was empty and our stomachs were so full
that we couldn't squeeze in another drop. It felt rather like
having swallowed a football. We tried to settle down to sleep
on the tarpaulins and flags spread out on the deck inside the
fo'c'stle for us, but the unaccustomed warmth became a stifling
heat; the vibration of the engines, the whole attitude of
relaxation and freedom to move around was so strange that
sleep would not come, exhausted as we were. I lay thinking
strange thoughts of the life in the sea, like a merman suddenly
abstracted from an environment which has become his own
and returned to a forgotten way of life amongst strangers. I felt
lonely for the sea and for the uncomplicated issues there at
stake, until I realised that my thoughts had for so long been
centred on devising ways to reach land that this unexpected
interruption of our plans, the destruction of our painfully
acquired stores of food and water, the sudden abrogation of the
survival laws, the tyranny of which still dominated our minds,
was all rather overwhelming and we would need a few days to
readjust to civilised channels of thought.

At about midnight, we could stand it no longer and staggered
out on deck to seek the cool night air, the starlit skies, and the
swell of the ocean. Robin, lucky man, was asleep. The junior
watchkeeper, Hidemi Saito, a personable young Japanese who
could speak one or two words in English, and had a phrase
book with the usual inappropriate situations, came up the foredeck and after enquiring the cause of our unease, brought us
our second meal, a noodle congé with small pieces of beef. The
flavour was enchanting! He then plied us with sleeping pills

which didn't make the slightest difference to our mental turmoil. Robin appeared just in time to finish off the remainder of the congé and we brought our pieces of bedding out on deck and rested under the stars.

In the days that followed we indulged in the luxury of eating and drinking wonderful food, the meals growing in quantity and sophistication. The familiar figure of the cook, Sakae Sasaki, became the symbol around which our whole existence revolved as he bore tray after tray up the foredeck to us. Spinach soup, prawns, fruit juices, fried chicken, roast pork, tinned fruit, fermented rice water, coffee and, a special treat, lemon-flavoured tea; and always in the background of our diet, like the foundation stones of a building, bread and butter. The assault upon our stomachs seemed unending and even when they were full, we still felt hungry—a most frustrating sensation! Our bones and bodies ached in contact with the unyielding deck, luxuriated in the deep hot sea water bath, groaned under the burden of indigestion, relaxed in the cool of the tropical night, and each day we gently exercised our swollen ankles and weakly legs, learning to walk again.

The Japanese crew took the twins to their hearts and showered them with kindness. They had already made gifts of clothing to us all, soap and toilet requisites, towels, notebooks and pens. They delighted in watching the twins draw, write and play together.

It took four days for *Tokamaru* to reach Balboa, by which time we had to some extent learned to use our legs again; in four days Captain Kiyato Suzuki and his wonderful crew brought the milk of human kindness to our tortured spirits and peace to our savage minds. They also removed the bitter canker of revenge from my character for when I had been a young man, my ship had been bombed and sunk by the Japanese war machine, and the memory of the screams of the trapped firemen in the stokehold and the flesh hanging in strips from the bodies of my friends had lived with me in bitterness through the years, through my later visits to Japan, and even through the rescue of my family and myself. These kindly fishermen were a new generation of men whose character bore no resemblance to the ogres in my memory, for they not only bore friendship to us,

Neil is carried ashore at Panama

but also to each other. Their humanity regained my respect for their nation.

If for no other reason than this one, the voyage of *Lucette* had been worth my while, but as we watched Douglas and the twins talking and drawing pictures with their new-found Japanese friends Lyn and I felt that they too had become citizens of the world, learning to communicate without the help of language, knowing that men and women of other nations and races had hopes, fears and ambitions which were not so different from our own.

We arrived in Panama at four o'clock in the morning and as *Tokamaru I* eased her way under the Bridge of the Americas and entered her berth in Balboa, the popping of flashbulbs from the cameras of the press, the shouted questions, and the rush and bustle of television and radio reporters thrusting microphones under our noses, made us wonder if the broad silent reaches of the Pacific Ocean were not to be preferred! An oasis of peace was imparted to us by the able management of the situation by Mr Daly, the British Consul in Panama City, and in his care and protection we were conducted through a short press conference and had photographs taken with our Japanese friends. Lyn and the children wept as they said 'Goodbye' in new-learned Japanese: 'Me-na-san, ka-za-ku, sy-an-ara.' (Thank you, we shall not forget, farewell!) The news fraternity, delighted to have this demonstration of emotion on our return to civilisation, allowed us to go in peace and we were whisked off to the large American-style Hotel Executive where we immediately resumed our pursuit of allaying the insatiable hunger of our bodies by the consumption of large quantities of steak and eggs, with pancakes and waffles on the side, and ice cream to follow. (Douglas and Robin had three breakfasts each that morning, only one of which was supposed to satisfy a rancher!)

Our medical examination, conducted with care by the staff of Santo Tomas Hospital, Panama City, found us to be anaemic (in spite of our bloodthirsty practices) but already recovering from the after-effects of severe dehydration (one of which is an inability to walk). Sandy had a slight bronchial pneumonia which was treated with antibiotics without requiring his admittance to hospital, and Neil had suffered more generally from the effects of dehydration than the rest of us. Our legs were subject to swelling if exercised too much and we were told to resume normal activity slowly. Blood pressures were not exceptional and pulse rates although high (90 to 120) were attributed to the strain and the overloading of our digestive systems, also to our continuing sleeplessness. (I could still only manage two hours a night.) We had all lost weight, between twenty and thirty pounds each, from bodies that weren't fat to start with, but this and subsequent examinations have disclosed no lasting ill-effects either external or internal.

During the ensuing days in Panama City we received cables and telephone calls from our friends and relatives from all parts of the world, offering and giving help to us in our time of need. It was an experience in friendship which completed the good work already started by our Japanese friends, and made our rehabilitation so much easier. Robin flew back to England ten days later and we boarded the MV *Port Auckland* in Colon the following day to return at a more leisurely pace. As we waved goodbye to the Jansen family, our good friends in Colon, we felt that a new world had opened before us, and that though *Lucette* was gone and our small savings with her, the wealth and depth of the experience we had gained could not be measured in terms of money.

# Coincidence

During the voyage to Balboa on board *Tokamaru* we talked with the Japanese in drawings, and by means of the phrase book, of our separate voyages, theirs from Japan, ours from Britain through Panama, and of the coincidence which had brought us together in the timeless wastes of the Pacific, a story in itself illustrating the occurrence of the improbable and confounding the expert. (Robin had never lost hope of being rescued, and I had calculated the chance of being rescued to be so small that it could be discounted. A case of the statistician adopting the attitude which rightfully should have been mine, and of my adoption of an attitude which ought to have been his!)

My mind went back over the sequence of events that had resulted in our course coinciding with that of *Toka Maru*. I thought back to the sinking of *Lucette* two hundred miles from Fernandina, and further back still to the departure from Panama three months previously, and the ensuing days of uneasy calm alternating with squall and thunderstorm when *Lucette* had made her way south and west through the Doldrums as wind and sea allowed, using the auxiliary engine to help the sails take advantage of the adverse winds. Strange sea creatures had swum close around us, giant turtles, shells four feet across, sharks, rays and snakes. On one occasion a whale as long as *Lucette* had cruised alongside us for half an hour, only a hundred feet away from us. As the huge bulk of the whale kept station alongside us, it became evident that it was eyeing *Lucette* with more than a passing interest, for on occasions it would roll over on its back exposing its pale yellowish underbelly in what my farmer's eye took to be a mating gesture. This behaviour pattern was repeated three or four times, the whale coming to the surface and blowing occasionally, the spray from its vent drifting across *Lucette* in an evil-smelling mist until Lyn, holding a handkerchief to her nose, shouted 'Go on the other side, your breath smells!' As if it had heard, the whale dived a

Galapagos Seal

little more deeply passing close under the keel and coming up on the starboard side, where the peculiar rolls were repeated, until, tiring of *Lucette*'s lack of response to this most pressing courtship, the whale dived steeply and disappeared. Robin, his seasickness forgotten for the moment, talked excitedly with Douglas and the twins until a heavier than usual roll upset his internal equilibrium once more.

After a week of alternate calms and squalls *Lucette* had finally entered the trade wind belt, the fresh breeze blowing steadily from the south, and closehauled she beat south-westwards to the Galapagos. On the fourteenth day out from Panama we sighted Marchena Island, and coasting round the strangely barren coastline of black lava, tacked southwards against wind and current, past San Salvador island and Santa Cruz to Wreck Bay, the port of entry for the Galapagos, situated on the western tip of Chatham Island.

Nine days later, after bidding farewell to our new friends Señor and Señora Garcia and their schoolteacher daughter Elizabeth, we had walked through the gardens of the Naval Establishment with its imposing statue of Charles Darwin, and out on to the stone jetty where Douglas manoeuvred the dinghy alongside the steps with great caution, for embarkation was difficult in the six-foot surge. With Lyn and myself safely aboard, he had sent the dinghy skimming across the harbour with powerful strokes of the oars to *Lucette* where our usual last-minute chaos was gradually resolving itself into the ordered appearance of a yacht ready for sea. Our departure was finally delayed by a neighbouring yachtsman, asking advice on the best route to Hawaii, so that it was late afternoon before we finally weighed anchor and sailed for Barrington Island, thirty miles distant. Dusk had fallen by the time the cliffs of Barrington were near enough to distinguish the detail necessary to navigate the tricky entrance to the only anchorage, so we stood off for the hours of darkness watching the luminous trails of phosphorescence made by the sea creatures playing around the hull. As daylight revealed the mysteries of the rocky coastline, so it concealed the identity of the living things in the sea, and it was not until a dog-like, bewhiskered face popped up near by that we realised that the marine inhabitants of the Galapagos were escorting us into harbour. With an ease which we had hitherto only attributed to dolphins, the seals dived and cavorted around *Lucette* as we steered through the entrance to the cove and anchored close to the white ketch *Albatross*, the only other occupant of the anchorage, while the seals lifted their graceful sea shapes on clumsy flippers and waddled up the rocks of the nearby island, informing their neighbours of our arrival with discordant, cow-like bellows.

*Ednamair* was soon lowered and Lyn and the boys explored the seal colony, scrambling over the cactus-covered rocks worn smooth where the seals had dragged their bodies to the sea. Large pelicans watched solemnly, unperturbed by the proximity to the boys when they went near to obtain photographs. Robin and Douglas then climbed the slopes of the main island to look for land iguanas while Lyn and I chatted to the owners of the ketch, old friends from Antigua. The twins after completing their essays on the journey through the islands went swimming with tireless energy in the cool Pacific waters; we had intended to look at Charles Island next, but our friends persuaded us not to miss Hood Island, so that night we weighed anchor and beat eastwards against wind and current hoping to make the next anchorage before dark, on the following evening. Douglas and

Robin described how they had seen and followed the land iguanas, large lizard-like creatures about three feet long with frilly combs down their backs, survivors from a prehistoric world, and had finally cornered them to be photographed. The slow-moving lizards, like the pelicans, were quite unafraid at the approach of humans. We arrived in Gardiner Bay with half an hour to spare, anchoring in the sheltered waters of a beautiful sandy beach, distant honking betraying the presence of another seal colony.

We scrambled ashore next morning, walking through the herds of seals lying sunning themselves on the beach and into the scrub-covered hillside behind. Mocking birds, finches and pigeons watched us curiously, quite unafraid, some even landing on us and picking at our clothing with lively interest, while red-throated lava lizards darted around in the rocks keeping a wary eye for the hawks circling high above us. Small snakes of a non-poisonous variety were quite numerous amongst the rocks and made us wary of treading on them. On our return to the beach we plunged into the sea to cool off, and while we could easily

Galapagos Penguin

outmanoeuvre the seals on land they now proceeded to show us who was master in the water. In groups of ten to twenty they swooped close by in the sea, leaping clear of the water at times and banking in circles around us like playful children. Only on one occasion did they touch us, one of them playfully nipping at Douglas's rubber flipper when he had dived towards it. Ungainly on land, they were as graceful as dancers in the sea and we never tired of watching them at play.

We then moved *Lucette* to the anchorage at the western point of Hood Island to allow us to visit the nesting places of the sea birds there, but first we met the island's sole human inhabitant, a very shapely one in the person of Dagmar, a blonde young German student, studying the life and habits of the lava lizard under the auspices of a Swiss university. She explained her work of recording the life of this hardy little lizard, and introduced her friends, the little finches and mocking birds all of which she knew by pet names. We crossed the island's rocky plateau, coming upon many gannet-like birds nesting among the rocks; these were the blue-footed boobies peculiar to the Galapagos, and spectacular divers when hunting fish. As we approached the weather side of the island, the great roar of breaking surf grew in volume, and salt spray drifted across the plateau, although we were two or three hundred feet above sea level. Sandy and Neil raced ahead after Douglas and Robin to the cliff edge and stood gazing in silent wonder at the awe-inspiring scene before them. Hundreds of feet below, the huge Pacific combers dashed their white fury against the rocks with thunderous roar, flinging spray high on to the cliffs behind. At frequent intervals a column of water and spray vented through a blowhole in the lava and shot hundreds of feet into the air, projected by the incompressible dynamism of the wave action. (What enormous resources of natural power and energy lie neglected and untapped, ignored by man's blinkered commercial vision.) The mist of spray drifted, glistening in the bright sunlight, over the black cliffs, a rainbow gleaming its spectrum colours across the sombre background of rock. Far below, seals flopped lazily around beside deep, sea green pools and scarlet crabs sparkled the black rocks like a primeval rash. Nearer to us, on a tower of rock isolated from the cliff, black marine iguanas lay piled on each other in motionless

heaps, intertwined like hideous black spaghetti, their dull
wrinkled skin and toad-like heads belonging to another era.
Over all, the gulls, frigate birds, petrels and boobies kept
constant vigil, swooping in graceful soaring flight over the blue-
green ocean.

If we had seen a prehistoric monster emerge from a cleft in
the rock none of us would have been surprised, but as it was we
were treated to the astonishing sight of a huge bird, curved beak

Waved Albatross

snapping and wings outstretched to a span of eight feet,
tottering on uncertain legs to the edge of the cliff where it
launched itself into space, gliding in a graceful dive to gain
momentum, then soaring high into the air to make for the open
sea. Hood Island is the only place in the world where the waved
albatross breeds and as we walked back through the scrub, we
saw many of them brooding their large single white egg, and
were even lucky enough to watch a pair perform their peculiar
mating dance; as the birds faced each other, wings dipping,
beaks snapping and feet dancing, their heads bobbing close
together in unison, we were vividly reminded of the nuptial
dances performed by the San Blas Indians.

Dagmar, returning from a fishing expedition empty-handed,
accepted our invitation to dine and we all listened, fascinated,
as she described her life and work on this lonely island; then

after seeing her safely back to her lizards and birds, we sailed at midnight for Fernandina, passing Post Office Bay on Charles Island (where the old barrel, used by the early whalers as a post box, still stands) the following afternoon. Around the southern tip of Isabela the next morning *Lucette* reached across the easterly breeze, past the barren coastline of cinder-like lava. Isabela is the largest of the Galapagos Islands, and here giant tortoises live in the craters of the extinct volcanoes, and more than one unwary explorer has found death, lost in the thick undergrowth of the arid mountainside.

Sperm whales spouted around us as we sailed northwards until the cone-shaped peak of a huge volcano loomed out of the haze ahead and the black forbidding mountain of lava slowly emerged to view, silhouetted against the setting sun; this was Fernandina Island. We anchored in an unnamed bay on the south-east point, the call of the seals and birds accentuating the loneliness of this black wilderness.

The dawn view of Fernandina had been breathtakingly beautiful in the rays of the rising sun; the green belt of vegetation around the volcanic peak shone like a jewelled collar above the forbidding black slopes of lava, thrown in tortured profusion by subsequent earth tremors, after the molten rock had hardened into petrified rivers.

We had pulled the dinghy well up into the narrow belt of mangrove trees, and setting a fairly modest target for our walk at one of the hillside craters, struck out across this wonderland of barren lava, finding to our surprise that where the surface had not been broken up by subterranean upheaval the going was quite good, and the lava skin unweathered after a million years of exposure, severe storms being unknown in these islands. Here and there a lone cactus stalk, like an elongated pincushion, held precarious root in the waterless surface of the lava but otherwise there was no vegetation, or moss, or insects or animals of any kind. As the sun rose in the sky, waves of heat emanated from the black lava surface, and we had soon modified and finally abandoned our objective, struggling back to the sea shore, footsore and weary in the blistering heat of the equatorial sun.

The twins, thankful to reach the sea again after our five-hour marathon, dashed from rockpool to cove, marvelling at the variety of fish life in the tidal pools, and the brilliantly coloured crabs around them. We carefully skirted the seal colonies, for many baby seals were being suckled under the mangrove trees and we did not wish to frighten them. When we reached the cove where the dinghy was beached, we plunged headlong into the sea without bothering to change, cooling off before a bright-eyed audience of flightless cormorants, pelicans, gulls and boobies.

A fine afternoon's sailing, beating into the fresh northerly breeze, had brought us off Tortuga point at dusk, and rather than risk the tricky approach to Espinosa in the darkness we had decided to stay in the deep-water anchorage of Tagus cove for the night. We tacked in towards the high mountains of Isabela, starting the engine as the hills deprived us of the wind, and motored slowly in through the gathering darkness. In starlit silence the hills closed around us, Douglas heaving the lead from the bows of *Lucette* and finding no bottom at a hundred feet, although we were close to the shore. (Our echo-sounder was working rather erratically and I preferred not to trust it.) The phosphorescence gleamed brightly around *Lucette*'s hull as she eased her way into the cove, the lead splashing showers of green sparkling fire as it struck the sea surface and plunged into the depths, until a shout from Douglas informed me that we had at last found the bottom. The darkness was intense so we lowered *Ednamair* and I sent Douglas and Sandy to sound out the cove ahead of us. Charts can be disconcertingly wrong at times. Finally under their direction we had dropped anchor a safe distance from the almost vertical walls of rock around us.

We had been awakened by Neil early next morning, excitedly shouting out yachts' names, and we had tumbled on deck to view this astonishing documentation of the cove's visitors over the past years. As I have already mentioned, Douglas added *Lucette*'s name to this distinguished gathering before we left for her appointment with destruction, although predestination would have to be a tortuous business indeed to have arranged our meeting with the killer whales to accord with the random nature of our cruise through the Galapagos Islands.

*Tokamaru I*, a three hundred ton motor fishing vessel, had left Japan on 4 April 1972, bound for the fishing grounds in the south Pacific, normally a round voyage of about three or four months. She had developed engine trouble and lain in Honolulu for forty-three days while the trouble was put right, then resumed her journey to the tunny fishing grounds about 8° south of the equator. Fishing had been slow, and finally running short of oil, she had been ordered to Manzanillo in Mexico to refuel.

*Tokamaru I* had already passed, unseen, well to the west of us when her orders were changed and she was instructed by her owners to proceed to Panama, thus bringing her on a convergent course with the *Ednamair*. Although we had already been spotted by the watchkeepers on the bridge it had been decided that a tiny craft like *Ednamair* couldn't possibly sustain life at that distance from land, and thus it was not until our signal was seen that in the words of Hidemi Saito, 'We dived for the automatic steering and came full speed to the rescue'. For those who believe that a higher intelligence directed the movements of our craft, there is much evidence to sustain their belief. For those on *Ednamair* who, like myself, simply believe that coincidence has a very long arm, we can but accept the fact of our meeting with *Tokamaru* with humble gratitude; but for that, the outcome of our ordeal, if for instance we had attempted to land in our weakened condition, could have been tragic indeed.

Part Four

# The Last Analysis

Much advice, many scientific assessments and a considerable amount of experience have been brought to bear on the subject of survival at sea. I am deeply disturbed by the continuing conflict of advice offered to the unfortunate people who find themselves, no matter how, in isolation from the rest of humanity and thrown upon their own resources in a small craft on the open sea. I therefore propose to offer a constructive criticism of our present techniques to assist survival with suggestions for their improvement, and at the risk of treading on some authoritarian toes, the referral to the laboratory of both old and new techniques for further testing before they are either finally discarded or accepted.

In the natural sequence of events, let us first consider the disaster. We are concerned here principally with the speed at which the parent craft is destroyed. If it is a gradual process and there is time to send out distress radio signals, and receive acknowledgements, the problems are simplified to surviving the disaster and staying as near to the stated position given as possible, until rescue is effected. The estimate of the extent of damage is important here, but should present no real problem to the competent commander. There will be adequate time to release the necessary safety apparatus and to ensure a plentiful stock of food and water before the parent craft is abandoned.

If, on the other hand, disaster is sudden and without warning, no radio message is possible except from emergency equipment already stowed in the life-saving apparatus, or from an automatic beacon, with which only the more sophisticated vessels are equipped. The range of such beacons, if adequate, usually gives only a vague estimate of the position of the survivors unless an accurate directional fix is obtained from other stations, so that no substantial reliance should be placed on immediate rescue. In any case, lives will depend on the state of readiness of life-saving equipment and on the quantity and type of stores already stowed within the environs of such equipment, or attached to it by an efficient line. Any type of equipment which has to be carried to the survival craft after it has been launched may have to be abandoned, and what may seem to be a simple operation, taking a few seconds under normal conditions, may be impossible to carry out under disaster conditions. Any equipment which requires assembling after disaster has struck must be considered inefficient.

The efficiency with which survival equipment is launched will depend upon the position in which such equipment is stowed and the ease with which it can be released under disaster conditions. Patent slips or slip knots should be used on all lashings and ease of access and release must be assured irrespective of the difficult angles at which the parent craft may sink. Level-headed action by everyone connected with the launching and storing of equipment within the survival craft should not be a prerequisite to survival, for even the most level-headed of operators, or passengers, can be unavoidably detained in the disaster area, or dead.

Level-headed action after the life-saving craft has been launched can contribute largely to increased chances of survival, and if time permits, increased storage of water, food and equipment should be undertaken from the parent craft if still above water, and from any debris left afloat. Surprisingly important uses can be found for apparently useless pieces of debris. Necessary precautions must be taken, however, if bringing debris aboard an inflatable raft and it is better to abandon an object if there is any risk of it piercing the raft accidentally, or of wearing holes in the fabric.

I think it is probably a help to others who are afraid, if one can conceal the outward evidence of one's own fear, but it is better to work quickly even if the appearance of haste gives the impression of fear if the loss of time also involves the loss of lives. Instant disaster allows no time for ponderous decisions and actions should be taken in their order of importance. Let me relate this statement to our own abandonment of *Lucette* to illustrate my meaning. Important time was wasted by myself in attempting to stem the influx of water into the yacht. The extent of the damage by one whale was irreparable and sufficient to sink us. We were hit by three. We had always kept a bucket of stores on deck for survival purposes. It had been emptied to help carry water supplies aboard and hadn't been refilled; the thought of stores was instantly in our heads but had we stopped to gather some, we would not have had time to release the survival craft. It was a matter of good luck rather than good planning that the right knife was available to us.

People do odd things in an emergency and we all have stories of ludicrous situations about which we laugh afterwards, if we are still alive. (My favourite one is of the third mate of a merchant ship who, after a tremendous explosion and thinking his ship had been torpedoed, leapt naked from his bunk and jammed both his legs down one leg of his shorts, so immobilising himself that he had to crawl out on deck on his hands and knees. Fortunately the explosion hadn't come from a torpedo but from a closely dropped depth charge.) In the case of *Lucette*, when I first shouted 'Abandon ship' from the cabin, Douglas ran to lower the sails while I was wasting time looking at the hole. Only Lyn reacted immediately with the correct action and then much of her contribution was wasted by thoughtless planning. The water containers, which she cut loose, sank because they were filled to the brim with no pocket of air left in to keep them afloat, and as I have mentioned the polystyrene icebox which contained five gallons of water floated away because it had no line attached and we were unable to go after it for fear of attack by the killer whales around us.

People panic in desperate situations because they do not know what to do and the soothing attitude by many operators of telling passengers as little as possible of survival arrangements is not only used to cover up inefficient arrangements but is positively disastrous in the event of the knowledgeable crew members being killed (as in an air crash). The contents of the emergency kits should be clearly listed on the outside of the appliances so that the operator may make up a satisfactory supplementary kit if he so desires.

In the last analysis, and this often is the last analysis, lives are saved because sufficient trouble has been taken to ensure the swift release of equipment and then lost because, after an efficient release, the equipment placed in the hands of the survivors is inadequate to sustain life. There can be no more

bitter betrayal than the discovery of inefficient life-sustaining
equipment after an escape from instant death.


### Stores

Let us now turn to the examination of the materials installed
in the raft or boat to enable the survivors to live until rescue is
effected. In traditional forms of life-saving craft, storage capa-
cities of food and water vary from three to ten days. Supplementary equipment in the shape of some form of rain-catcher, a
few fish hooks and some line, first-aid equipment, etc., varies in
proportion to the craft supplied and is often virtually useless
when operated in unfavourable conditions; these conditions
usually exist in survival craft.

Let us firstly examine the simple problem of water, the most
important constituent of the survival stores. There has been a
considerable amount of experiment, carried out under practical
and hazardous conditions, to demonstrate that sea water may
be used to supplement the diet of castaways. While I do not
wish to detract in any way from the achievements in other fields
of survival technique which some of these experiments have
reaffirmed, this particular aspect, namely that of drinking sea
water, requires that the castaway should not be dehydrated
when he drinks it. Why, then, should he drink it at all? 'To
alleviate the castaway's despair,' says one authority. The suggestion that a castaway should stop alleviating his despair when
he feels the need for the substance he is using to allay it is a
useless nonsense, and I propose to show by quoting from actual
shipwreck experience that there is indeed nothing to be gained,
and much to lose, from following this most dangerous advice.
I quote on the next page the official British position on this
matter as set out in a notice to masters, officers and seamen
of merchant ships:

## BOARD OF TRADE
## MERCHANT SHIPPING NOTICE No. M.500

## DRINKING OF SEA WATER BY CASTAWAYS

Seafarers are reminded that if castaway they should NEVER UNDER ANY CIRCUMSTANCES DRINK SEA WATER which has not been through a distillation plant, or de-salinated by chemical means.

A belief has arisen recently that it is possible to replace or supplement fresh water rations by drinking sea water in small amounts. This belief is wrong and DANGEROUS.

Drinking untreated sea water does a thirsty man no good at all. It will lead to increased dehydration and thirst and may kill him.

Even if there is no fresh water at all it should be remembered that men have lived for many days with nothing to drink, and therefore the temptation to drink untreated sea water must be strongly resisted.

Board of Trade                                        MC 54/09
Marine Division, London
November 1965
Reprinted March 1968

Since the castaway has to adopt some personal attitude to this argument perhaps our experience can be of some assistance to him in arriving at a decision. All evidence, from both sides of the argument, points to the fact that if the body of the survivor is at all dehydrated, sea water can not only cause damage to internal organs and sickness, but it will intensify the dehydrated condition. Most advocates of the sea water theory qualify their advocacy by stating that it can only be usefully assimilated by a body that doesn't really need it. During the periods of severe thirst when we were on raft and dinghy, Lyn and Douglas both admitted to an almost overwhelming desire to drink sea water, both by day and night. Only their own moral fibre prevented them from doing so, but how much would that moral fibre have been weakened if they had drunk some sea water in the initial stages after the disaster? I cannot emphasise

too strongly that survival conditions are not the same as those
voluntarily undertaken by brave men who wish to help survivors fight for their lives. The physical conditions may be quite
similar, but the moral incentives, the attitude of experimental
interest as opposed to that of escape from catastrophe, can alter
a person's judgement of what is right or wrong and this difference can kill!

Perhaps the following excerpt from Richard Hakluyt's
*Principall navigations . . . of the English nation* (1589) may help
to illustrate what comfort the real castaway derives from the
practice. The disaster occurred when the *Delight*, with Richard
Clarke, master, had been destroyed after striking the shoals off
Sable Island, near Newfoundland. The date was 21 August
1583, and although the weather was bad, conditions were
probably suited to a low rate of dehydration by loss of body
fluid, so that the survivors from this shipwreck would not be
immediately subject to the severe thirst which quickly develops
in those survivors castaway in tropic zones.

And when the shippe was cast away the boate was asterne
being in burthern one tunne and an halfe: there was left in
the boate one oare and nothing els. Some of the company
could swimme and recouered the boate and did hale in out
of the water as many men as they could: among the rest they
had a care to watch for the Captaine (Maurice Browne) or
the Master: They happened on my selfe being the master,
but could neur see the Captaine: Then they halled into the
boate as many men as they could in number 16, whose names
hereafter I will rehearse. And when the sixteene were in the
boate, some had smale remembrance, and some had none:
for they did not make account to liue, but to prolong their
liues as long as it pleased God and looked euery moment of
an howre when the Sea would eate them vp, the boate being
so litle and so many men in her, and so foule weather, that it
was not possible for a ship to brooke halfe a coarse of Sayle.
Thus while we remayned two dayes and two nightes, and that
wee sawe it pleased God our boate liued in the Sea, (although
wee had nothing to help vs with all but one oare, which wee
kept up the boate withall vpon the Sea, and so, went even as
the Sea would driue us) there was in our companie one

Master Hedely that put foorth this question to mee the master. I do see that it doth please God that our boate lyueth in the Sea, and it may please God that some of vs may come to the lande if our boate were not ouer laden. Let vs make sixteene lottes, and those foure that haue the foure shortest lottes wee will cast ouer boord, preseruing the Master among vs all. I replied vnto him saying, no, wee will liue and dye together. Master Hedly asked me if my remembrance were good: I answered I gaue God prayse it was good, and knewe how farre I was off the lande, and was in hope to come to the lande within two or three dayes, and sayd they were but threescore leagues from the lande, (when they were seuentie) all to put them in comfort. Thus wee continued the third and fourth day without any sustenance, saue only the weedes that swame in the Sea, and salt water to drinke. The fifth day Hedly dyed and another moreouer: then we desired all to die: for in all these fiue dayes and fiue nights we sawe the Sunne but once & the starre but one night, it was so foule weather. Thus we did remaine the 6 day: then we were very weake and wished all to die sauing only my selfe which did comfort them and promised they shoulde come soone to land by the help of God: but the company were very importunate, and were in doubt they should neuer come to land, but that I promised them the seuenth day they should come to shoare or els they shoulde cast me ouer boord: which did happen true the seuenth day, for at eleuen of the clocke we had sight of the land, and at three of the clocke at afternoone we came on lande.

Richard Hakluyt, *Principall Navigations, Voiages and Discoveries of the English Nation* (1589).

Estimates vary as to the length of time the human body can remain active when water is not available. Obviously the period varies with climate and with the sort of care taken to avoid activity in excessive heat, but we managed to remain coherent and active for periods of up to a week on less than a third of a pint of water a day each. The constant soaking of our skins with sea water probably helped a great deal, but in any case, there is no real danger that the castaway will die from water shortage (even if he has no supplies) in the first three days which seems to be the period in which sea water drinking is championed. Until more conclusive proofs of benefit are forthcoming I would therefore recommend that sea water should be considered poisonous.

Alternative sources of water can be derived from rain, fish, or as in our case, turtles. Rain has to be caught and stored. I have not seen an efficient rain-catcher, but I am sure that it is not beyond the ingenuity of man to devise something like a blown-out umbrella which could be expanded by an umbrella-like mechanism, held in the appropriate position by one man while the water runs down inside the stick into the waiting receptacle. When all the receptacles were full it could then be used as a shelter by readjusting the angle of the spreaders. The material used would have a polished impervious surface so that no water is retained in the material, avoiding a preliminary 'washing off' period should the rain-catcher be soaked with sea water. Small rain showers can make valuable contributions to water reserves in this way. In our case, by the time the surface of the catchment material was free from salt, the shower had passed away, and subsequent soakings in spray polluted the material again before the next shower. Proper receptacles should be provided in the equipment. These should be of tough material which will not split when stood on, or lain upon, and should be provided with a small spout for accurate pouring in heavy seas. Water tins should be non-rust and provided with caps so that they can be re-used without having to remain upright (a most difficult balancing feat in an inflatable raft!)

The administration of water by enema was probably a great help in speedily alleviating the dehydration suffered by us in times of drought. While we used water that was unpalatable, it was not undrinkable. I had wondered if it would be possible to use sea water in this way, but Lyn had strongly advised against it. Sea water taken by enema would cause as much damage as if it was taken by mouth. (This proves that my wife is wrong and that I do listen to her sometimes!) Robin, who refused the enemas, showed no particular disability because of it, unless his delirium could be regarded as a sign that he was perhaps more dehydrated than the rest of us.

Fish are a useful source of water and while we can all

stomach raw fish if need be, it sometimes takes more effort to catch than to eat them. The particular fishing line which was supplied with our equipment, and which I so stupidly threw away, would have proved virtually useless anyway in the light of subsequent losses of far stronger line. In fact, the constant presence of sharks makes line fishing an uncertain business, for, as many sport fishermen know, a shark will quickly attack and devour a captive fish struggling at the end of a line, and in all probability it will take the line too. Line fishing in temperate waters may prove more successful, but in our situation the gaff was undoubtedly the answer. If water is to be extracted from fish, and there are a number of survivors to be fed, then one cannot do with one or two flying fish although these are welcome titbits. Fish have to be caught in quantity and with certainty and the gaff is the only sure way to bring them aboard, even when they are brought within reach by line. A gaff with a small hook is probably the best type for an inflatable raft for the hook can then be buried in the fish while bringing it over the flotation chamber and thus be less danger to the raft itself. We did not feel much of the sense of alleviating thirst by eating the raw flesh of fish (except the Mako shark) but certainly sucking out the spinal fluid was a great joy, as were the eyes; two pounds of fish contains about a pint of water. Some fish may be speared with a sharply pointed knife and although I did catch one or two small scavenger fish in this manner, I was always unhappy about holding the precious blade over the side of the dinghy. I feel certain that an attempt to spear the large dorado with it would have resulted in its loss. Given a strong enough gaff, the attraction of the dorado by the distribution of a suitable bait to excite the smaller fish should ensure an adequate supply of fish for any number of castaways. In cases where dorado are not available and surface fish absent, the use of metal spinners is less likely to attract the attention of sharks than fresh bait but, in any case a steel trace should be affixed between hook and line to prevent the line being bitten through. If a shark has to be brought in on an inflatable I should recommend it be brought over the flotation chamber tail first on its back, a paddle thrust in its mouth at the earliest opportunity and the fish held until it is dead; the jaws may then be cut out and thrown over the side before the fish is dressed, for it must be remembered that

one slash by even a dead shark's teeth would open up an inflatable as if cut by a surgeon's knife. If the shark is a large one, cut
the line and let it go.

The turtle was the mainstay of our existence, although if they
had not been available we would have tried harder for other
fish. They are powerful swimmers and can inflict a painful bite
to the unwary hunter as well as cause damage by their lacerating claws. It may be as well to use ropes to secure them in the
first instance, but it must be remembered that they can bite
through a rope. Once aboard and laid on its back a turtle is
helpless but not harmless; determination and a sharp knife to
the turtle's throat soon turns the situation in the castaway's
favour but it is essential to ensure that the main blood supply
is tapped to achieve speedy results. The collection of the blood
is quite easy if the spurting blood vessel can be directed into a
cup but the blood must be drunk immediately for it coagulates
in about thirty seconds. There is no particular taste that I can
remember except that it seemed deficient in salt rather than
the reverse. Once I had taken the first cupful and declared it
good stuff, the others drank it without much trouble and both
Robin and Douglas quite liked it after the idea of drinking it
was accepted. There have been prior instances of castaways
drinking turtle blood although I had not heard of them at the
time. As a matter of interest I quote the following extracts from
*The Voyage of the Resolution and Discovery 1776-1780*, edited by
J. C. Beaglehole (1967). The incident happened after Captain
Cook had discovered and named Christmas Island. The first
extract is from Cook's journal:

> In the afternoon the boats and turtling party at the SE part
> of the island all returned on board, except a seaman belong-
> ing to the Discovery, who had been missing for two days.
> There were two of them at first, but disagreeing about which
> way they should go, they seperated and one joined the party
> after being absent twenty four hours, and very much dis-
> tressed for want of water; in order to allay his thirst, he killed
> a turtle and drank of its blood, which gave him great reliefe,
> the other man could not drink of it and was of course in still
> greater distress, for not a drop of fresh water was found on the
> whole island nor were there any cocoanuts in that part.

And the following is from the journal of David Samwell, one of the ship's surgeons:

> . . . they had mistaken their way in bringing Turtle across from the Sea Beach to the boat, and had been in the utmost Distress for want of Water. After trying several times in vain to procure water by digging wells in the sand, they had recourse to drinking the Turtle's blood, flowing out of the wound they cut in his Throat, which instead of quenching their Thirst made them sick; they found most benefit by plunging themselves frequently into the Sea . . .

None of *Ednamair*'s crew was sick as a consequence of drinking turtle's blood; we were, like one of Captain Cook's men, afforded 'great reliefe'.

There seems to be some doubt as to whether turtle livers are really injurious to health and on the principle of our abstention from sea water, turtle livers should also be left strictly alone until more substantial proof of their goodness is forthcoming.

In the course of discussing water supplies a lot of the ground was covered which would normally be included under food, and since this is a less important aspect of survival than water I shall here only refer to the more vital stores which should be included in the castaway's emergency rations. Obviously the supply of proteins and fats will be adequate if fish are caught in large amounts. The supplementary vitamins, trace elements and carbohydrates are not in such sure supply so that a store of these should be given priority. Multivitamins and iron, in tablet form, and glucose in hard sweets, are more suitable than the powdered forms of these substances. Hard biscuits to nibble are a great comfort, but crumbly substances and powders are to be avoided since they are difficult to divide and distribute without loss. We all enjoyed a lick of dried yeast off a wet finger end, for as long as it lasted.

Salt may be an odd thing to discuss at this time but deficiency of salt causes many ailments in hot weather and the supply of salt necessary to the body forms the basis for arguments in favour of drinking small quantities of sea water. Salt is lost from the body by sweating and in the urine. If sweating and urination are much reduced through low intake of water and

minimum activity, the intake of salt should also be reduced. At
sea level, moisture particles in the air, particularly if the sea is
disturbed, carry a considerable amount of salt which is automatically ingested while breathing. Now the sort of conditions
in which increased salt intake is necessary are associated with
heavy sweating and an intake of eight pints of fresh water daily;
these conditions will obviously not exist on survival craft, particularly crowded survival craft. It only remains for me to say
that at no time did we feel a need for salt, nor did any of us take
salt water deliberately.

If there is any space left in the food locker after these essen-
tials are stored, beef extracts or yeast extracts last a long time
and a little goes a long way. Milk tablets too would be a most
useful addition if space can be found.

The other equipment in the survival craft apart from the
means of propulsion and the rain-catcher (with containers)
should include very strong fishing lines, traces, hooks and
spinners, a gaff as already mentioned, a spear head (largely for
protection), a useful knife, a first-aid kit with a castaway's
ailments in mind, and a gentle reminder that the metal articles
should be non-ferrous. (The most useful tool we had was a pair
of rusty artery forceps. We discovered turtle oil too late to save
them.) Other items which should be included are a good bailer
which can also be used as a urinal, drinking vessels, and where
necessary a very efficient repair kit, which would contain epoxy
resins as well as hull-repairing materials, something to sharpen
the knife on and plenty of small line. Sea anchors, although
bulky, are essential. All the above articles should, if possible, be
made to float. It would be a useful addition to an equipment kit
if an intelligent handbook were included, telling the castaway
what he needs to know, rather than what he ought to do. Some
instruction books are great morale boosters, causing castaways
to fall about with laughing by the time they finish reading
them. Things like putting three days' food and water in the
stores and then telling the castaway to be careful with it for he
might be on the raft for twenty-one days. Or packing eighteen
pints of water, supplies for ten persons for three days at two
pints a day each. This exercises the castaway's mind especially if
he doesn't have his personal statistician along to reassure him
that he isn't barmy. There are so many ludicrous statements

made in these books that one is tempted to look askance at the useful information that they contain, on principle.

The navigational equipment (we didn't have any!) should be waterproof. A clock and compass, with luminous dials, dividers strong enough to be used as small fish spears, and a world series of charts showing shipping lanes with frequency of use, ocean currents with set and drift, seasonal weather with, most important of all, rainfall expectations; these make an engrossing study for a castaway and the knowledge that he can drift a thousand miles in fifty days can make him decide to try to do just that rather than accept the inevitable alternative.

A bird chart may also prove a useful addition to a castaway's 'library', so that he can determine the presence of land birds. It would also serve to prevent false hopes being raised if a reasonable assessment of the range of sea birds from land could be included in the chart.

There have been many attempts to place reliance on bird life as a sign of proximity to land, and while it is generally true that the nearer land is approached, the more markedly the variety of species and number of birds increase, the rule can only be adhered to very loosely and many exceptions make this feature merely an aid rather than a navigational rule.

I have noticed tropic birds four hundred miles out in the Atlantic from Barbados, and if they can travel as far as that, they can go much further. Boobies, frigate birds and shearwaters may also be seen many hundreds of miles from land and petrels and albatross seem to range at will. Land birds sometimes fly well out to sea after losing their way, or can be carried over large distances in the eye of a tropical storm. Yachts and ships have been visited by very small land birds two hundred miles out to sea so that their presence cannot be interpreted as a sign of nearby land. If the castaway sees a number of land birds flying around, which don't take the opportunity of landing on his craft for a rest (and he is not on an oversea migration route), he may reasonably hope that land is near, but if the other signs like floating vegetable debris, stationary cloud, smell, discoloration of water are absent, then the presence of land birds should be noted with interest, not conviction.

The last item of equipment I wish to mention is as important as the first, signalling equipment. At night the modern types of flare and rocket give a good visual indication of the castaway's whereabouts. By day, orange smoke signals are probably best. Supplementary to these are, of course, a good torch with spare batteries and bulb, and a heliograph. The whole success of a signal revolves largely round the question 'Is anybody looking?' On many occasions during the voyage of the *Lucette* I was forced to alter course, under sail and in difficult circumstances, to keep clear of other vessels when it should have been my right of way even as a steam vessel. What chance has a castaway of being seen by such a vessel, unless he happens to be in possession of a rocket which he could fire at it? It seems to me that the advent of radar, gyro and autopilot, especially the last, has brought about a situation both in steam and sail which behoves ill for future castaways, and promises to increase their numbers to a considerable degree. Ample comment has been made on this subject by learned and influential bodies connected with the sea and to their pleas for sanity I would only add these words. Every time a seaman hears about, or reads about, or actually sees, a castaway, he should say to himself: 'There, but for the grace of God, go I.' To be at sea without a proper lookout is a wilful neglect of one of the basic tenets of good seamanship. Steam and sail alike.

### Action

The castaway has managed to escape from his sunken parent craft and now sits, in a severe state of shock, reading his handbook and examining the small defences which lie between him and death. If he survives the reading of his handbook and the examination of his stores, he has to decide his best course of action. This is usually a life or death decision too, so it shouldn't be taken lightly. (At this stage for no specific reason, I am reminded of a friend in Miami, who, aggrieved that he hadn't read about our catastrophe in his newspaper, phoned them up and was told: 'People are always doing this sort of thing, just so they can get in the paper!')

In our case we had four options. The one we took; the return to Galapagos; the impossible voyage to the Marquesas; or to 'stay put'. We seriously discussed the chances of two of us setting out in the dinghy to try to make it back to the nearest village, about two hundred and fifty miles up wind and current, but rowing non-stop at two knots against a current of one and a half knots would have meant that we would cover ground at about twelve miles a day, it would have taken us over twenty days with no prospect of water, and if we had failed those who were left behind would have died too. Since no estimate I have heard of puts a man's survival beyond ten days even with very limited quantities of water, any attempt to reach the Galapagos was almost certain to fail. The remaining alternative, that of staying put, I have already discussed adequately at the beginning and would only add that a small radio telephone, battery operated, could make staying put a feasible plan, if contact were made and the prospect of rescue thereby assured. In all other cases the survivors should start immediately to make plans for a journey to the most suitable land; this may not necessarily be the nearest, or even the easiest, but it will afford a reasonable chance of regaining civilisation. Remember that it is easier for exhausted castaways to travel by sea than by land, and to destroy one's craft making a useless landing on an uninhabited island which won't support life, or on a part of the coast which is cut off from habitation, is to waste the effort expended on reaching it.

The enormous difference between actively fighting for survival and passively awaiting rescue or death effects a complete change in the castaway's outlook; he becomes master of his fate and will devise means to survive which no textbook can prescribe for him. The best assistance he can be given is good information and reliable material, the rest is up to him, and with sufficient determination he will succeed.

### Craft

I do not propose to recommend or condemn any type of survival craft, for anything is better than nothing. There are ways, however, in which the castaway can prolong the life of his craft if he is given adequate information about this in the beginning.

Inflatable craft, for instance, are usually made of some sort of waterproofed fabric and in consequence, when people are living on the fabric, and continually moving around, it is naturally subject to wear. When the fabric rubs itself constantly against neighouring fabric through wave action, it wears, often in places where the damage is undetected until it is brought to the castaway's attention by an influx of water or a collapsing flotation chamber. Manufacturers should be at great pains to make these areas of wear as strong as possible, for their customers' lives depend upon them, and they should also take immediate steps to remove any ropes which may fray the surface of the fabric. The floors of inflatable craft should also be protected from the attacks of predators, perhaps by a simple baffle sheet, both for the comfort of the occupants and the durability of the craft. The weakness of the fabric joining flotation chambers and flooring can, by leaking sea water into the raft, cause the castaway long hours of pain through the development of salt water boils, which create unbelievable agony for the sufferer when they are knocked, and on a crowded raft this happens fairly often. Once this particular section of the flooring is holed there is nothing the castaway can do to repair it.

Bellows supplied in the inflatable kit should either be reliable and of good quality, or else the manufacturer should simply include a pipe with a suitable mouthpiece, through which the castaway may top up the air pressure by blowing. Anything in between is a downright mockery! The sort of repair kit supplied to the castaway should enable him to effect repairs at sea, without having to use precious fresh water to clean salt out of the fabric, and it would be a considerable step in the right direction if when all else had failed, he was able to inject some sort of solidifying foam into a chamber to render it serviceable.

There are many advantages to inflatable craft and for these the castaway is suitably grateful; I am quite sure the manufacturers can look after this aspect of information without my help, but I would add that having had two types of inflatable craft in my experience, the aforementioned weak points were common to them both.

The dinghy which has to serve the double purpose of lifeboat and tender has the initial advantage of a hard durable outer skin and the disadvantage of having less inherent buoyancy than the inflatable. As a rule, inherent buoyancy can only be increased at the expense of internal capacity unless the dinghy is of the double-skinned variety. (In this type care must be taken to ensure that the outer skin is not punctured since there is no visible outward sign to indicate this.) In either case, additional buoyancy in the form of a flotation collar of a solid buoyant material adds considerably to the safety of the castaway

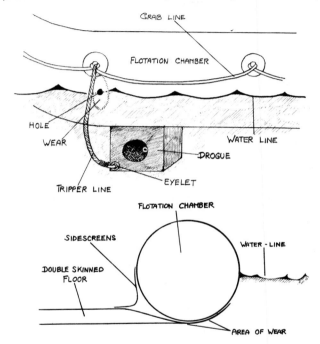

Areas of wear on inflatable: at water level (*above*) and at floor level (*below*)

and his craft, especially in the event of swamping. As a rule, yacht dinghies have a cutaway stern to accommodate an outboard motor and in consequence of this they are unseaworthy when stern on to the weather in ocean conditions. If, however, they are fitted with a jury rigged square sail and made to sail stern first, presenting the most seaworthy part of the craft to the approaching seas, they perform the function of a lifeboat in a much more satisfactory manner, and in order to make this backward progress more reliable, a drogue of some description, streamed from the bow, will be of immense help. *Ednamair* sailed over seven hundred miles in this manner. (The dinghy may be steered across wind in the manner indicated earlier on, provided the seas are not too rough.)

Canopies perform most useful functions in all types of craft, bearing in mind that ease of exit in the event of a capsize in bad weather is of the highest priority. (Careful attention to the sea anchor can minimise the risk of a capsize in any craft.)

### *Personalities*

The personalities of the castaways often come in for a lot of scrutiny when survival issues are discussed. High-sounding phrases about leadership, duty and discipline are very impressive in instruction books; the perils of boredom, apathy and (good heavens!) idleness are emphasised as well. In real terms, knowledge is leadership, common sense is duty, and the practical observance of survival laws is discipline; any departure into the realm of orthodox authority at this stage is specious nonsense, and the crass idiocy of creating work for 'idle' hands should be instantly exposed as such. There is usually plenty of time for discussion about policy decisions and if people know why they are doing a thing it helps them to do it.

The system of self-rationing which we used for saving water was much more successful than imposed rationing could have been, and I'm pretty sure that most castaways would have behaved similarly in the circumstances. Rationing, imposed in our case for reasons of ensuring that everyone took their ration of water, used the reserves up much more quickly. Self-denial lies at the very core of moral strength and moral strength motivates the castaway in his determination to survive. There will be lapses from this harsh code of behaviour but they are soon restored with the help of one's comrades, and the spirit of comradeship is a far more important factor in survival than any imposed discipline. It is the spirit of comradeship which enables the castaway to suffer extremes of discomfort and even to offer life itself to assist the survival of the others. The lone castaway is, in this respect, at a grave disadvantage. Discomfort is a devastating destroyer of morale and only a deep understanding of the need to share discomfort will reconcile the sufferer to pain and prevent him from attempting to better his lot at the expense of the others. Comradeship is a ready substitute for this understanding.

In our case, Robin probably suffered more than any of us in this acceptance of the survival laws. He barely had time to recover from his initial seasickness before he was abstracted from the civilised, stylised behaviour of student life and thrust into the melting pot of practical application. Where we others (twins as well!) had learned to live with the sea and with the harsh laws of survival on the farm, they must have come home to Robin with savage cruelty in their naked alternatives. Added to this his loneliness in the midst of our long-standing family attachments created agonies of indecision before he was able finally to abandon the carefully fostered prejudices acquired in the course of his education. Survival is the hardest school in life; there are no failures.

If any single civilised factor in a castaway's character helps survival, it is a well-developed sense of the ridiculous. It helps the castaway to laugh in the face of impossible situations and allows him, or her, to overcome the assassination of all civilised codes and characteristics which hitherto had been the guidelines of life. A pompous adherence to precedence, an assertion of physical superiority, the inability to abandon prudish reserve, these and many other such traits are as deadly as thirst and starvation in the confines of a survival craft. A recognition that this is so helps castaways to adjust to the realities of their position.

Lyn's adjustment to survival was made so much easier for her by the deep knowledge and experience of life and death situations which she had acquired in her nursing career. Her agony and desperation as a mother watching the swift deterioration of her children could only detract from her personal ability to cope, and I believe that her spiritual beliefs would have resulted in her death if the burial at sea of any of our children had been necessary. (I am not discussing these beliefs in themselves, only how they affected survival.) She resented it deeply when she noticed that I gave Robin larger portions of food than Douglas or myself, even after I had explained my motives in doing so, and her spirit of self-sacrifice was so dominant that it was through fear that she would be the first to die (with the terrible consequences that this would have had on the twins) that I insisted on introducing water rationing to ensure that she took her share. She did not really believe that we could reach land, until during the last two weeks when our food and water reserves accumulated in sufficient quantities to make the remainder of our journey feasible. Her worst moments occurred when she realised we could not return to the Galapagos Islands; when she thought that I would not succeed in reaching the dinghy when it broke loose; and when we transferred from the raft to the *Ednamair*. She still thinks that her premonitions of disaster were valid. (She told Douglas once that she dreamt that we were all sailing on the sea in a ham tin. When we went over to *Ednamair* from the raft, Douglas said to her: 'Well, mother, here's your ham tin!') Lyn is quite convinced that a spiritual presence assisted us in the storm, and that her prayers were more effective than her prodigious feats of physical endurance and concern for our creature comfort, to say nothing of her expert nursing care. She also, and with the feminine illogicality which I wouldn't dream of questioning, assures me that the only reason we were all saved was because the *Lucette* took with her the baby's caul, which she had saved from one of the deliveries in her midwifery days.

Douglas's worst moments were during the first two days when he did not believe it was possible for us to reach rain in time; or indeed that we would reach it at all. After we had rigged the dinghy and had completed our first day's run successfully he realised it could be done and immediately felt a changed man. Despite the terrible disappointment of missing the ship (he felt at the time that it had deliberately ignored us) his fear of death by dehydration only reinforced his determination to take advantage of every means of survival open to him. He didn't mind Robin having a little more food, but resented that he couldn't share more in the work. Douglas took more work off my shoulders as time went by until he performed most of the heavier tasks of hanging the meat, raising and lowering the sail, extracting the flipper bones of the turtles, besides a multitude of smaller tasks like sharpening the knife, and checking lashings and sail fastenings. He also had ideas of making nets from sailcloth to strain plankton from the sea, but this never became necessary. I could not have been blessed with a better assistant. His experience has not made him afraid of the sea, and as I write Douglas is concluding his negotiations to serve a four-year cadetship with a major oil tanker company.

I would hesitate to ascribe independent thoughts to the twins and would not attempt to determine how much their presence made our survival necessary. Their influence on our adult behaviour undoubtedly increased our tolerance of each other and the simple fact of their presence prevented differences of opinion, discomfort and the unbalanced share of work from escalating into something more serious. Neil felt happier in the inflatable and Sandy felt better in the dinghy. They weren't quarrelsome at any time and although reluctant at times to exercise their limbs, they always took an interested part in the work of the boat and the catching of food. They didn't think of dying when Lyn was trying to assuage their fears by explaining that they might, if they had no water, go into a long sleep; they thought she meant just that. Looking back on their experience, they thought it was rather exciting and in fact, two days out from Liverpool on our return to Britain, Neil, bored with the shipboard routine, said 'I'm fed up, Dad, I wish we were back on the raft!' They both have expressed similar sentiments since!

Robin never doubted that we would reach safety, and felt that we were capable of existing indefinitely on *Ednamair* until rescue or landing was effected. His sense of security grew rather than diminished as time went by and his confidence in our ability to support ourselves from the sea and reach safety was unshaken. His worst moments occurred when I took the decision to abandon the raft for *Ednamair*, my fear that we would be unable to trim the dinghy efficiently enough to prevent swamping communicating to him (as I had hoped it would). As he became accustomed to living in the dinghy he not only regained his confidence in our ability to survive but it grew stronger as our food and water position improved. He did not think of our vulnerability after the flotation collar was destroyed, and only became aware of the danger after we had been rescued. At the time of our rescue, he had grown accustomed to the whole idea of living from the sea even though, in practical terms, he would have been unable to do so.

Those are a few of the thoughts and feelings of the survivors from *Lucette* given to me after their safe return to land. My own feelings, fears, hopes, despairs and joys are strewn all along the pages of this book, where I shall let them rest in peace.

I cannot conclude these remarks on personalities without commenting on a friend's suggestion that Robin must have suffered more than the others because of his height in the cramped conditions of raft and dinghy. This was not so. I cannot imagine anyone with sharper elbows, bonier knees or hornier feet in the whole of Wales, and when they were applied to the more tender parts of our boil-infested anatomies, the suffering was scarcely mutual.

There is another aspect of a castaway's feelings which I haven't yet touched upon but which is dear to the hearts of fiction writers. I refer to the spine-chilling, blood-curdling, terrifying, gruesome desire to eat fellow castaways; in short, cannibalism. It is difficult to imagine the circumstances at sea under which one castaway would consider eating another, raw, for where water is in short supply, hunger is not the most pressing aspect of the castaway's needs, indeed where thirst is dominant hunger is absent. If water is plentiful, the personality of the castaway would require to undergo major changes before he could bring himself to eat his companion, and the change would be away from the characteristics which enable a man to fight other species for survival. His spirit of competition would be directed against his fellow castaways with consequent strife and self-destruction. If thirst-quenching blood is the object of the cannibalism then the cannibal is wasting his time. The salt content of the victim's blood will be as high as his own and he will derive no benefit from it. If the victim is the weaker of the two, the salt content of his blood will be higher and the cannibal would risk death by drinking it in the same way that he would by drinking sea water.

Like the fiction writer, I can imagine the frightful deterioration of character which would lead a castaway to serious thoughts of eating his fellows. Such a character, in my estimate, would merit restraint, by any means, to avoid credence in his ideas, and also to demonstrate most forcibly the unbalance of his mind.

### *Enemies*

Over the years there have been many reports of large fish attacking yachts, small boats and rafts. Many times the *Ednamair* and our inflatable raft had the appearance of being attacked by large sharks as they rushed towards us, only to skim underneath, often scraping their fins or bodies on the hull. I could never quite make up my mind whether they were trying to brush parasites from their own bodies or, in view of the number of sucker fish clinging to the bottom of our craft, trying to snatch a tasty titbit, and bumping us in the process. These sharks, often longer than our boat, did us no deliberate harm that I could see, but their harsh skins probably caused serious wear to the fabric of the inflatable, and the danger of one of them capsizing the dinghy made us very uneasy so that we quickly prodded them away. I always felt nervous when dumping blood, offal and shells from the turtles, especially with the inflatable around, but we suffered no deliberate attack as a result although we could see the sharks cruising near. Large sharks often leapt clear of the water, presumably striking at other fish, for the leap wasn't repeated as when trying to shake off a parasite, and I feel that a human struggling on the surface, as in fast swimming, is much more likely to suffer attack from a hungry shark than if he is quiet and wary. The sharks we encountered were mostly of the recognised man-eating varieties, the White-tipped, the Hammerhead and the Mako. On two occasions Douglas saw a Blue shark but to my knowledge and relief, although we had no means of knowing their colour at night, we did not encounter the White shark, the most voracious of the species. It is to the White shark that most small boat attacks by sharks are attributed and these beasts should be discouraged by all means available. Even though these attacks have taken place, I feel tempted to place them in the category of marine vandalism, rather than that of a deliberate attempt to obtain food by upsetting the boat, and this is borne out where the occupants weren't eaten, nor the boat actually destroyed in a sustained attack.

While discussing the vagaries of the different varieties of shark and their actions I do not feel the sense of awe that comes to me when the word whale is mentioned. Quite large vessels have been attacked and destroyed by various sorts of whales and I feel it is important to examine the possible reasons for some of these attacks. A recognition of the nature of the whale may help in determining the reason for the attack, so let us start with the largest, the Blue whale. This mammal lives by extracting tiny organisms from plankton, the basic food on which most marine life depends, either directly or indirectly. In common with all the lesser plankton eaters these huge beasts, growing to over a hundred feet long, are normally docile and in so far as their fellow mammals are concerned, quite harmless. The exception to this rule could occur if a boat were struck in error, which is most unlikely; in anger, when the whale itself is attacked; or in what I imagine the one really dangerous situation to be when, during a mating sequence, a bull whale mistakes a yacht for a rival. The mistake made by the female (I think) Sei whale on our voyage from Panama to the Galapagos Islands could have been difficult for us if there had been a belligerent bull around, and there are records of yachts being destroyed in apparently unprovoked attacks by whales, and of whales being destroyed in head-on collision with large ships: to act in this way from sheer bad temper would be out of character for these beasts.

There are other varieties of whales which live by eating fish and squid and the largest of these is the Sperm whale, many of which are found in the Galapagos area. These whales dive to enormous depths in pursuit of their quarry and although they are credited with a fearsome talent for destruction when attacked (like that of Moby Dick), the only dangerous situation to a yacht, apart from a jealous bull, could occur in situations like that of one unfortunate yachtsman sailing through the night who rammed an apparently sleeping whale on the surface. Deeply chagrined at this rude awakening the whale cruised round in a large circle and rammed the yacht, sinking it. Fortunately the incident occurred close to land and the yachtsman was able to escape, the whale having no further interest in the matter.

It is at the lower end of the weight scale that the Killer whale enters the list, the adults being a mere three tons or so, but significantly, they top the list in a different category of predators.

They are the largest carnivora on Earth and their natural prey are warm-blooded animals like seals, porpoises and whales. Like other carnivora they indulge in widespread killing and as a fox will indulge in a murderous orgy of killing if it gains access to a hen house, such is the behaviour of the Killer whale amongst a herd of seals. They hunt in packs and their victims,

30-foot Killer Whales

large and small alike, are paralysed with fear at the imminent attack and offer no resistance.

An increasing number of these voracious killers are held in well-fed captivity in aquariums throughout the world; they learn to do clever tricks, and although one or two have been remiss enough to close their jaws on a trainer, it seems the occupation is no more hazardous than say, lion taming, and as long as the whale is not hungry it might let the trainer go again. I have no argument with these captive specimens who are as like the hunting Killers as the captive wolf is to the hunting pack. Indeed, we may find a valuable use for them.

While a large whale would make a good meal for a pack of Killers, it has been firmly established that there is enough room

inside just one Killer whale to accommodate the whole
Robertson family and Robin as well. There are no records, that
I know of, which establish a firm intention in Killer whales to
destroy yachts and obviously *Lucette* was a case of mistaken
identity, else we should not be here to tell the tale. It is a matter
of deep concern to me, however, that while the whale population has been decimated by man, in some cases almost to the
point of extinction, the Killer whale population remains largely
unchanged since they are more difficult to catch and not so
profitable to process. By nature's law they must adapt in order
to survive, and if they can attack one yacht in error, the error
may be repeated many times as they are increasingly deprived
of their natural prey. In many cases we shall never know, for
the unfortunate yacht and its crew will simply disappear without trace. It would be a catastrophic development to the
yachting fraternity if even the odd Killer whale discovered that
tipping up boats was a good way of obtaining a meal, so it
might be a good idea to learn what stimulates the Killer into
attack (apart from hunger that is!) and what can be done to
deter it. The captive whales have a prominent part to play
here, and if some enlightened authority could inaugurate the
necessary experiments it may result in a useful defence mechanism being established before the need for it becomes tragically
obvious.

In the case of *Lucette*, I was tempted to consider the colour of
the anti-fouling bottom paint as the source of attraction, in
view of the attention paid to us by the Sei whale after we left
Panama, but it would seem that the bellies of whales and porpoises vary widely in shade and colour according to species and
all are prey to the Killer. If the shape or the speed of the hull is
important in stimulating attack, it may be possible to develop
some sort of oscillator to baffle their system of echo-detection,
but unless it worked continuously, its effectiveness would
depend on the efficiency of the lookout. Until some sort of
defence mechanism is developed, it seems that yachts and boats
will be subject to attack by these ferocious beasts, whether in
error or not is hardly important once the attack has been
pressed home. When this happens I have only one course of
action to recommend. Don't waste time looking at the hole, or
tuning a radio. Get your survival craft over the side first, then

do what you can before your yacht sinks; it could be that you have time for nothing else.


My story has run full circle, having started and finished with the destruction of *Lucette*. I suppose that, had we not survived, we would have vanished without trace as others have done before us, with hardly a ripple to show in the maelstrom of world events. It would probably have been pointed out to our grieving relatives that in a fifty-year-old yacht anything can happen, and only the few who knew her would have paused and wondered. My heart still grieves that her fine hull was so wantonly destroyed, and I am grateful that she took as long as a minute to sink; other yachts of more modern build would have succumbed in much less time, taking their unfortunate crews with them.

In spite of my scanty appreciations of her crew I will go on record now, saying that I could not have been castaway with five more tolerant, stout-hearted people, bonded together with love of life and ready to sacrifice it for each other; but for them, it would have been so easy for me to die with *Lucette*.

| SHARKS. | WHALES |
| --- | --- |
| WHITE | BLUE |
| BLUE | SPERM |
| WHITE-TIPPED | SEI |
| HAMMERHEAD | KILLER |
| MAKO | |